GOLF

by.

Bob
Rosen
or
Barney
Rubble

PHYSICAL EDUCATION ACTIVITIES SERIES

Consulting Editor:

AILEENE LOCKHART
University of Southern California
Los Angeles, California

Evaluation Materials Editor:

JANE A. MOTT
Smith College
Northampton, Massachusetts

ARCHERY, Wayne C. McKinney
BADMINTON, Margaret Varner Bloss
BADMINTON, ADVANCED, Wynn Rogers
BASKETBALL FOR MEN, Glenn Wilkes
BASKETBALL FOR WOMEN, Frances Schaafsma
BIOPHYSICAL VALUES OF MUSCULAR ACTIVITY, E. C. Davis,
    Gene A. Logan, and Wayne C. McKinney
BOWLING, Joan Martin
CANOEING AND SAILING, Linda Vaughn and Richard Stratton
CIRCUIT TRAINING, Robert P. Sorani
CONDITIONING AND BASIC MOVEMENT CONCEPTS, Jane A. Mott
CONTEMPORARY SQUARE DANCE, Patricia A. Phillips
FENCING, Muriel Bower and Torao Mori
FIELD HOCKEY, Anne Delano
FIGURE SKATING, Marion Proctor
FOLK DANCE, Lois Ellfeldt
GOLF, Virginia L. Nance and E. C. Davis
GYMNASTICS FOR MEN, A. Bruce Frederick
GYMNASTICS FOR WOMEN, A. Bruce Frederick
HANDBALL, Michael Yessis
JUDO, Daeshik Kim
KARATE AND PERSONAL DEFENSE, Daeshik Kim and Tom Leland
LACROSSE FOR GIRLS AND WOMEN, Anne Delano
MODERN DANCE, Esther E. Pease
PHYSICAL AND PHYSIOLOGICAL CONDITIONING FOR MEN, Benjamin Ricci
RUGBY, J. GAVIN REID
SKIING, Clayne Jensen and Karl Tucker
SKIN AND SCUBA DIVING, Albert A. Tillman
SOCCER, Richard L. Nelson
SOCIAL DANCE, William F. Pillich
SOFTBALL, Marian E. Kneer and Charles L. McCord
SQUASH RACQUETS, Margaret Varner and Norman Bramall
SWIMMING, Betty J. Vickers and William J. Vincent
TABLE TENNIS, Margaret Varner and J. R. Harrison
TAP DANCE, Barbara Nash
TENNIS, Joan Johnson and Paul Xanthos
TENNIS, ADVANCED, Chet Murphy
TRACK AND FIELD, Kenneth E. Foreman and Virginia L. Husted
TRAMPOLINING, Jeff T. Hennessy
VOLLEYBALL, Glen H. Egstrom and Frances Schaafsma
WEIGHT TRAINING, Philip J. Rasch
WRESTLING, Arnold Umbach and Warren R. Johnson

PHYSICAL EDUCATION
ACTIVITIES SERIES

GOLF

VIRGINIA LINDBLAD NANCE
Class A Teaching Member,
Ladies Professional Golf Association
Formerly, University of Southern California

ELWOOD CRAIG DAVIS
San Fernando Valley State College
Emeritus, University of Southern California

Illustrations by **FRANCILE OTTO**

and

VIRGINIA LINDBLAD NANCE

SECOND EDITION

WM. C. BROWN COMPANY PUBLISHERS
Dubuque, Iowa

Printed in the United States of America

Contents

Preface

This book has been written to serve as a supplement to golf instruction. It is based both on our experiences in teaching thousands of men and women to play golf and on the responses of golf instructors in many schools and colleges. This revision continues the purpose of the original book: to illustrate, describe, explain and emphasize the fundamentals of golf and, thereby, to help the performer to achieve more consistent success. By reorganizing and revising some of the text, revising and adding illustrations and including additional and important material, we hope this edition more nearly achieves the original goal.

The organization and sequence of the ten chapters and their contents reflect modern principles of perceptual-motor learning, and also reflect our confidence in the good judgment, maturity, and ability of the reader. The first chapter is concerned with general orientation to the game of golf, to the clubs, the course and scoring. The reader is then introduced to his most important lesson—safety. The following five chapters present instruction arranged in order of significance and difficulty of mastery. The execution of special shots is considered in Chapter 8 while the following chapter presents additional help for the general improvement of the reader's game. The last, and very important, chapter considers those essential rules, knowledges and practices which govern golf and the points of etiquette which so greatly enhance the enjoyment and spirit of the game.

Because the authors feel that an abbreviated history of golf must necessarily fail in giving even an adequate appreciation of the heritage of personages, events and times related to the game, they refer the reader to a full and authoritative account, such as that presented in a standard encyclopedia.

This revision continues the intentions of the original book: to provide a source of basic instruction to supplement that of the teacher; to help and encourage the player to form important "mental pictures" by the use of illustrations; to suggest items for discussion and questions regarding play; to challenge the reader with typical examples of kinds of understandings and levels of skill that he should be acquiring as he progresses toward mastery of the game. In short, it is our hope that through these pages we may help the reader-player to live up to the challenges of "The Measure of a Golfer."

The Game of Golf 1

Golf is different things to different people. To some of the millions who play this game, it offers a chance to exercise in the outdoors. To others it means meeting people, companionship, sociability, or a way of relaxing and having fun. Still others learn golf because it is a professional or business asset, because one's family or favorite person plays it, or because of its popularity in conversation and in the mass communications media.

Wherever one lives in the U. S., a golf course can be found not far away. Each course presents different kinds and degrees of challenge. And, as one learns the game one joins others who accept that challenge, who enjoy it and with whom he can share his enthusiasm.

Here is an activity that is deceptively simple in appearance. It constantly asks to be conquered, yet never is. In spite of this, or because of it, golf is played by people of all ages, at every level of ability. Almost every person anticipates with pleasure the chance to learn golf. This feeling persists and serves him well as he goes through the throes of learning and as he continues to improve.

The Game

The object of golf is to play a round, usually 18 holes, in as few strokes as possible. At the beginning of each hole you are allowed to tee the ball so it is slightly elevated from the turf. After you strike the ball from the tee, you must then play the ball as you find it, (See Chapter 10, golf rules) and continue doing so, in your turn, until you hit it into the hole (cup) which is sunk in the carpet-like area called the putting green. The position of the hole is marked by a flagstick and usually the number of the hole is indicated on the pennant. You record your score for each hole on a score card, total the scores for each 9 holes, and then total these for your 18 hole score.

The Golf Course

Golf holes are measured in yards and these yardages are shown on the score card. Whenever you play golf you have a "universal" opponent —par. Par scores are good scores. The major guide for determining par for a hole is the distance of the hole. The number of strokes a good player needs to hit the ball onto the putting green is figured, and then two strokes are added for play on the putting green. Since women cannot hit the ball as far as men, women's par is higher than men's par.

On what may be called a regulation golf course, the holes vary in length from near 100 to near 600 yards. Courses having all short holes, near 100 yards, have become popular recently. These courses offer advantages to the novice. A simpler version of golf is played, thus more success and pleasure are possible for the beginner. These short courses are challenging, offer practice in the short game, and require less time to complete a round.

Much expert knowledge and work go into building and maintaining a golf course. Sometimes the game is so absorbing and exasperating that the beauty and design of a golf course are forgotten momentarily. Golf requires the largest playing field of any modern game. No two courses are alike. The architect designs the course to challenge you to hit your best shots and to penalize you if you do not. He lays out the course tak-

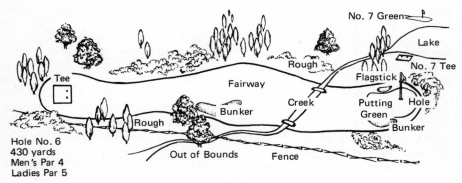

Figure 1—Golf Hole

ing full advantage of the topography, the beauty of nature and the outdoors. Golf is not all of life, but to have the opportunity to play outstandingly beautiful golf courses enriches life for an increasing number of people.

	COMPUTATION OF PAR	
Par	*Men*	*Women*
3	up to 250 yards	up to 210 yards
4	251-470	211-400
5	471 and over	401-575
6	-------------	576 and over

PLAY U.S.G.A. RULES except as modified by Local Rules										Please Observe Rules of Golf Etiquette												
HOLE NO.	1	2	3	4	5	6	7	8	9	OUT	10	11	12	13	14	15	16	17	18	In	Total	Hdcp.	Net
YARDS	525	415	390	167	560	430	185	380	440	3492	490	385	158	510	423	190	370	400	428	3354	6846		
MEN'S PAR	5	4	4	3	5	4	3	4	4	36	5	4	3	5	4	3	4	4	4	36	72		
MEN'S HDCP*	11	5	15	7	9	1	13	17	3		10	16	14	8	2	12	18	6	4				
Won + Lost — Halved O																							
LADIES' PAR	5	5	4	3	5	5	3	4	5	39	5	4	3	5	5	3	4	4	5	38	77		
LADIES' HDCP*	5	13	1	17	3	11	7	15	9		8	12	18	6	16	4	14	2	10				
Replace Divots and Repair Ball Marks on Green																						
SCORER.................................. ATTEST.................... DATE..................																						

SCORE CARD

Figure 2—Sample Score Card

*HDCP. is the abbreviation for handicap. It indicates the ranking of the golf holes in order of difficulty. In the sample score card above, hole #6, HDCP. rating #1, is considered the most difficult hole for men. Hole #3 is rated the most difficult hole for women. Holes #16 and #12, HDCP. rating #18 for men and women respectively, are considered the least difficult.

The Golf Clubs

You will face a variety of situations on the course. The distance you must hit the ball will vary from less than an inch to as far as you can hit it. You may play the ball from a beautiful grassy area, bare ground, sand, deep grass and weeds, behind a tree, under a bush, a deep gully, a hillside, and water, such as a creek—if you choose to do so. The rules allow you to carry a maximum of 14 clubs to make these different shots. Not all players use the maximum set. Players using 14 clubs do not all select the same clubs; however, the usual maximum set consists of 1 putter, 9 irons, and 4 woods.

The Putter—This club is carried by every golfer, and it is the one club used most. You use the putter to roll the ball relatively short distances into the hole. It is used on and from near the putting green. The putter has a short shaft and an almost vertical face. Aside from these two points there is a great variation in the design and construction of putters. The heads may be of metal or wood and of various shapes; the shape of the grip may be different from the standard grip of clubs; and the shaft may be attached to any part of the clubhead.

The Irons—The popular matched set of irons is made up of eight clubs, numbered 2 through 9. The #2 iron has the longest shaft and the least loft to the club face. As the number of the club increases, 3, 4, 5, etc., the shaft decreases in length and the angle of loft of the club face increases. There is, therefore, a great variation in the length and the trajectory of the golf shots made with different irons. There is about a 10 yard differential between irons. If you can hit a 5-iron 130 yards, then

RULE SITUATIONS—Hole #6 (See Figure 1)

1. In the address you accidentally knock the ball off the tee.
2. It appears your drive from the tee has rolled out of bounds.
3. Your 2nd shot is lost in the lateral water hazard.
4. In playing your 4th shot from a sand trap, you accidentally ground the club.
5. Your 3rd shot is lost in the creek crossing the fairway.
6. Your ball lies against a bridge crossing the creek.

Where should you place your golf bag or cart before putting?

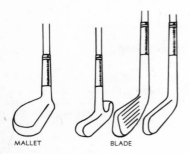

Figure 3—Types of Putters

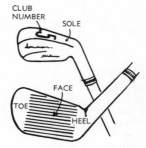

Figure 4—Parts of Clubhead

you can figure that you will hit a 4-iron 140 yards, and a 6-iron 120 yards. A special iron, a wedge, with a heavier flange and greater loft than the #9 iron is included in some matched sets. If the wedge is not included in the matched set, the experienced golfer usually adds this club or a similar one to his set.

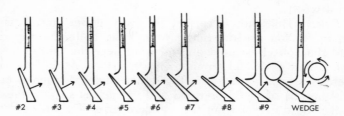

Figure 5—The Irons

The Woods—Matched sets of woods are made up of four clubs, either the numbers 1, 2, 3, and 4 or 1, 3, 4, and 5. The wood clubs are longer than the irons so you can expect to hit the ball farther with these clubs than with the irons. Like the irons, the woods vary in length and club

face loft. The near vertical face of the driver almost restricts its use to
hitting the ball from a tee. There is approximately a 10 yard distance
differential between the woods.

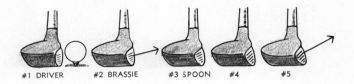

#1 DRIVER   #2 BRASSIE   #3 SPOON   #4   #5

Figure 6—The Woods

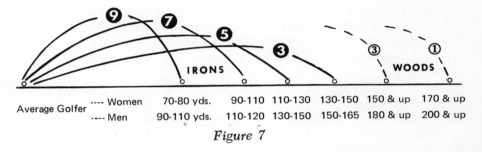

Average Golfer	---- Women	70-80 yds.	90-110	110-130	130-150	150 & up	170 & up
	---- Men	90-110 yds.	110-120	130-150	150-165	180 & up	200 & up

Figure 7

Beginner's Set—An excellent set of clubs for the novice consists of
seven clubs: putter, the number 3, 5, 7, and 9 irons, and the number 1
and 3 woods. A five club set, eliminating the #1 wood and the #9 iron,
also makes a suitable set for the beginner.

2 Safety—
Your Most Important Lesson

Considering the number of people participating in golf, relatively few accidents occur. When accidents do occur, however, they can be serious. Most result from carelessness and lack of knowledge. You have a responsibility for your safety and the safety of others. Learn the following rules and *take no chances where safety is concerned.*

1. If you are a member of an instructional class, follow the precautions given you.
2. Before you swing any club, check to see that no one is within range of your swing.
3. When someone swings a club, be careful where you stand or walk. Stay well out of range of any swing.
4. Do not swing a club so the follow-through is directed toward anyone. It is not likely to happen, but the club could break or it could slip out of your hands.
5. Do not stand or walk ahead of a player taking a stroke that may endanger you. Similarly, when you are hitting a ball that could endanger someone, see that no one stands or walks ahead of you.
6. Before playing any stroke on the course, make certain the group ahead is out of range of your intended shot.
7. If you hit a ball that is travelling toward someone and may endanger that person, call "FORE!" loudly so he will be alerted.
8. Stay on the tee line at the practice range. Do not walk ahead of the line to retrieve balls or tees.
9. When someone is teaching you or you are teaching someone, stand opposite the person, facing him. Do not stand on his right or left side in the path of the swing.
10. Lightning storms are dangerous on the golf course. The best precaution to follow is to avoid playing when such storms occur. Detailed precautions for protection from lightning when out on the course are given in the U.S.G.A. rule book.
11. If you use an electric cart to drive around the course, drive with care.

Many people carry personal liability insurance for protection in case accidents do happen. The protection offered by these policies may merit your investigation and consideration.

With knowledge and common sense, golf is a safe game.

On Learning Golf 3

The Ability to Imitate

You cannot help but use your ability to imitate in learning golf. You will "absorb" to varying degrees the golf swings you see. Imitation can be either an aid or a hindrance to learning. Young people, especially, imitate easily and to a high degree. Unlike some adults, they do not imitate on the intellectual or analytical level, but rather on a "subconscious" level. There is a quick grasp of the *movement as a whole*. Pictures and feelings are registered, but not in words. Many caddies and young people have imitated fine golf swings, and this imitation has played a part in their developing into good golfers.

Whether or not you possess a great deal of imitative ability, you can learn to make the best use of that which you have. Just as important, you can avoid complicating your learning by poor imitation. When you watch a golf swing, do not look for or try to copy small points of style, minor details of motion, or mannerisms and idiosyncracies. Keep in mind that *the golf swing is one motion*. If you see and have a "feel"* for the whole of a good swing—its design, pattern, rhythm, timing, power, and ease—then imitation can be an aid to learning.

The "How" of Swinging a Golf Club

The beginning adult student of golf wants to know "how" to swing a golf club. This too often means he wants to know all of the intricate details of the swing—the complex analysis of the whole movement. Even if such an analysis were possible, then what? It takes about two seconds to make the golf swing. How much can one think about and then translate into action in that amount of time? Skillful movement is beautiful and complex, a real accomplishment. Lucky for us that we do not have to send conscious messages to all body parts, and at the correct split second, to make a golf swing. If this were necessary, no one could execute a satisfactory swing. Yet, this is what some beginners think they must do.

Questions of whether the swing is natural or unnatural are meaningless. The golf swing has been learned and executed well by people of all ages—even by those with physical handicaps. Some people experience difficulty in learning the golf swing, but this is not due to the movement.

---

*Kinesthetic sense.

7

Trying to execute the "how" of the swing by performing numerous *details* of action is one of the chief reasons for problems in learning. Trying to think of and perform many parts of the swing in two seconds is not only impossible but also frustrating and tension producing. Discomfort, irritation, and exhaustion are some of the results, but not learning golf.

Overemphasizing one physical detail of the swing also causes trouble. For example, no one will question that the left arm remains fairly straight during a golf swing (putting excepted). The cue "left arm straight" is one of the most famous "hows" of executing golf swings. When this cue is carried beyond the correct position of *easy extension* to a stiff, tense position, learning the whole swing is not only difficult but almost impossible. Remember: your objective is to develop a golf swing—*a whole unit of motion*—not just a detail, and not a succession of details.

A good golfer performs details of action to which he has never given any thought. These actions are the result of swinging the club to stroke the ball to a certain position. *The purpose of the movement is an important factor in determining the pattern and form of the motion produced.* Suppose you wish to throw a ball straight up into the air. With this as the purpose, the arm swings up sharply and the body weight shifts upward with the arm motion. This coordination happens naturally. You neither think of swinging your arm up nor do you think of shifting your weight upward. You think about throwing the ball straight up into the air. If you thought of and carefully concentrated on the details of what the body and its parts do, would you be more effective in throwing the ball skyward? Keeping the objective of golf in mind—*stroking the ball to a target*—will help you develop the golf swing. Many of the details that you may now think are necessary "hows" of the swing will occur. They will *take their places as part of the whole swing*, as you concentrate on swinging to stroke the ball to a target. In learning the golf swings, do not only try to intellectualize the process. Place some trust in your body's ability to take care of details. *Permit learning to take place.*

Mechanics of the Swing

Incorrect information or lack of information of certain mechanics of the swing misleads not only the beginner but also the experienced player. This discussion presents certain fundamentals of the movement of the club and its contact with the ball. The purpose of discussing these mechanics is to prevent incorrect concepts and thus incorrect efforts. The correct basic concepts of clubhead motion and ball contact serve as a base for learning and developing an effective golf swing.

Clubhead Speed—It is a great pleasure to hit a golf ball a long distance—the desire of all golfers. But this desire has ruined many golf swings because of wrong attempts to get distance. The important factor in determining the distance the golf ball will travel is the speed of the clubhead at ball contact. This speed is directly related to the size of the arc of the swing. When you wish to stroke a ball a short distance, you choose a short club, grip down on the handle, and take a short swing. When you wish to stroke a ball a long distance, you choose a long club, hold it at its full length, and take a full swing. The clubhead will travel at a higher rate of speed in the full swing, and thus the golf ball will travel a greater distance. With the longer clubs you should hit the ball longer distances, but this does not always happen. Why? If you are not getting greater distance with a longer club, then you must be doing something to *prevent* the clubhead from developing its maximum speed at contact with the ball. Usually the fault lies in incorrect muscular *exertion.* Preparing to "hit hard" and exerting yourself with sudden and violent efforts at ball contact result in less clubhead speed and loss of control of the club. The timing and smooth blending of forces that come with correct muscular effort, together with the size of the arc of the swing, produce clubhead speed and distance. Do not be misled into thinking that it is recommended that you swing slowly when you take the full swing. The opposite is recommended. Let the clubhead speed develop—do not prevent it through exertion that could be better used for lifting a piano.

The Pattern of the Swing—If you consider two movements with which you are familiar, then the arc of the swing may be better understood. Assume you are going to throw a baseball underhand. What path does your hand take? It swings up as you swing your arm back in preparation for the throw. Then after the release of the ball your hand swings up on the follow-through. You do not think about and try to swing your hand *up.* This was a *result* of your purpose—not your purpose. Now assume you are going to bat a baseball. In preparation for the hit, you swing the bat in an arc back around you. On the follow-through after striking the ball, the bat again swings in a circular arc around you. You do not make any special effort to swing the bat in an arc.

In the golf swing you have a combination of these two arcs because the ball is on or near the ground. The swing of the clubhead upward and around you is again the *result* of your purpose. The circular pattern is a natural result of your standing in a fairly fixed position to strike the ball from the ground to a target. The arc is not something you set out to copy exactly. (See Figure 8)

Figure 8—Front and Side Views of Full Swing

Through the contact area the clubhead travels close to the ground. Because the clubhead travels in an arc around you, it enters the contact area from inside the intended line of flight, travels on the intended line of flight, and then on the follow-through again travels inside the intended line of flight. This is the natural outcome of a good swing. (See Figure 9)

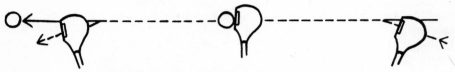

Figure 9—Arc of Clubhead Through Contact Area

Ball Contact—The direction and flight of the ball can be directly related only to the contact of the club face with the ball. Other factors may affect this contact, but they in themselves do not propel the ball—only the club face can do that. If at ball contact the face of the club is travelling on the intended line of flight and the face is at right angles to the line, then the ball will travel straight along the intended line toward the target. The two factors determining the direction the ball will travel are (1) the path of the clubhead and (2) the position of the club face in relation to the path of the clubhead. (See Figure 10)

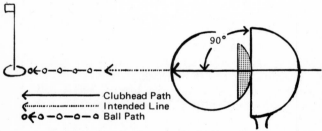

Clubhead Path
Intended Line
Ball Path

Figure 10—Impact Producing Straight Shot to Target

When you studied the pictures of the wood and the iron clubs, you learned an important fact. The loft of the club face determines the trajectory of the ball in the air. You do not attempt to hit the ball into the air—the club face is designed to do this. It is common to hear a struggling golfer complain: "I can't get the ball into the air." When you understand that the club face—not a special effort on your part—lofts the ball into the air, you have taken a *giant* step in learning golf.

A small error in contact with the ball may cause a great error in shot result. Golf requires a high degree of accuracy. You will get various shot results in your early attempts to strike the ball. This should not discourage or frustrate you. Considering the size of the golf ball and the small hitting area of the club face, the wonder is that so many fine golf shots are made.

Progression in Learning the Swings

If you have watched champion golfers prepare to play a round of golf, you have observed that they start their practice using the medium or short irons. They hit shots requiring less than the full swing and then work to the longer swings and the longer clubs. This makes sense. The short swing is an important stroke of the game. The "feel" and touch for all golf swings is best found and recovered in these short strokes. Short swings serve as easy muscle and joint "warm-up" for the full swing. These statements may be used to support the opinion: *if* it is best to start learning golf with a particular swing, then the choice should be the small swing. It is not suggested that the beginner delay working on the longer swing and the full swing but a little patience is recommended—walk before you run. You are apt to have more success in striking the ball with the less complex short swing than with the full swing. Success in striking the ball makes learning more enjoyable as well as more effective. The putting stroke can be learned and practiced right along with the other strokes.

The Real Secret

Useful guides can be given for learning golf and executing the swings, but no exact fomula can be proposed. Who can confidently say he has all the answers to learning golf or to consistently hitting fine golf shots? The novice watches the champion, notes a detail of the swing, and hopefully thinks he has "'discovered the secret" of good golf. You can be sure the champion does not want to know *this secret!* The champion already knows the REAL SECRET—hitting thousands of golf balls in practice and play.

4 Addressing the Ball

Taking the correct grip and the proper stance are the essential preliminary steps in executing successful golf shots with the irons and the woods. Some golf shots may be hit well when it appears that the fundamentals of grip and stance are defied, but defiance of the fundamentals only serves to tear apart a golf swing, because compensations must be *constantly* made to counteract errors. Your objective is to develop a sound swing and game that will improve with practice. Give yourself the best chance to do this. Start with the correct grip and stance.

The Grip

Types of Grip—The *overlapping grip* is the most widely used. In this grip, the little finger of the right hand rests on or overlaps the index finger of the left hand. In the *interlocking grip* the little finger of the right hand and the index finger of the left hand interlock. One advantage of either of these two grips is that there is a feeling of unity between the hands because of the overlapping or interlocking of the fingers. An advantage claimed for the overlapping grip is that you have both index fingers on the shaft. The index fingers along with the thumbs are key fingers in holding anything. A person with small hands and short fingers may prefer the interlocking grip. Various names have been given the grip in which all the fingers of both hands are placed on the club. One claim made for this grip is that it is a strong one. The person who lacks some grip strength or who has small hands may find the 10 finger grip most suitable.

Individual preference, "feel," strength, and the size of hands may all be factors in choosing the best grip for you. It is important to note that the three grips are very much alike; the only difference between them is the placement of the little finger of the right hand and the index finger of the left hand. All of the three grips have been used successfully, however, the overlapping grip is favored by the majority of golfers.

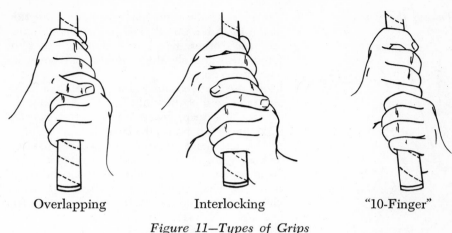

Overlapping   Interlocking   "10-Finger"

Figure 11—Types of Grips

Taking the Correct Grip

1. Place the sole of the club flat on the ground and support the handle with your right hand.
2. Let your left hand hang at your side. Note the natural hanging position of the left hand and arm.
3. Without changing the natural position of the left hand, move it forward to the club so that the club handle extends across the middle section of the index finger and back across the palm. The hand, arm and shoulder should still be in an easy, relaxed position.
4. The back of the left hand faces the intended line of ball flight. Be certain of this. Do not have the back of the left hand facing the ground with the palm pointing skyward.

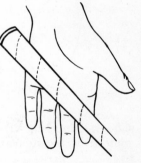

Figure 12

5. Keeping the left hand in the same position and relaxed, now close the fingers and take hold of the club handle. Hold the club with some firmness, but not with great tension. Holding the club with the left hand, you should be able to move the clubhead easily. Try moving the clubhead just a few inches back and forth on the ground while maintaining this correct grip.
6. Now, let the right arm hang easily at your side. Note its natural hanging position.
7. Without changing the natural hanging position of the right hand, move the hand to the club so that the club handle lies across the middle part of the index finger. The life line of the right palm is superimposed over the left thumb.

Figure 13

Taking the Correct Grip

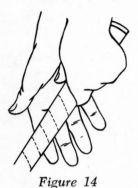

Figure 14

Figure 15

8. The palm of the right hand faces the direction of the intended target. The palms of the hands face each other. Be certain of this. The right hand, arm and shoulder should still be in an easy position.

9. Close the fingers and palm of the right hand and take hold of the club. If you are taking the overlapping grip, *let* the little finger of the right hand fall naturally over the index finger of the left hand. If you are taking the interlocking grip, raise the index finger of the left hand and interlock it with the little finger of the right hand. It is important that you do not change the positions of the hands when you overlap or interlock the fingers.

10. Check the face of the club to see that it is *square* to the intended line of ball flight. Check the firmness of the grip and ease of motion by moving the clubhead a few inches back and forth along the ground.

*Check Points—Left Hand—*Take hold of the club, look down at your grip, and check the following points. (See Figure 16)

*Figure 16
Lefthand Grip*

1. The V formed by the thumb and index finger points in the general area between the chin and the right shoulder. Checking where the V points is a matter of judgment. Follow your instructor's specific instructions.

2. The base segment of the thumb will touch the side of the hand, forming a line.

3. The left thumb is slightly to the right of the center of the shaft.

4. The knuckles at the base of the first two fingers can be seen, and perhaps the knuckle at the base of the third finger.

5. The tip of the thumb and tip of the index finger will lie close to each other.

Check Points—Right Hand (See Figure 17)

1. The V formed by the thumb and index finger points in the general area between the chin and right shoulder. See left hand grip.
2. The base segment of the thumb will touch the side of the hand, forming a line.
3. The thumb is placed slightly to the left of center of the shaft.
4. The knuckle at the base of the index finger can be seen, and perhaps the knuckle at the base of the long finger.
5. The tip of the thumb and the tip of the index finger lie close to each other. The tip of the thumb does not extend down the shaft beyond the middle joint of the index finger.
6. The left thumb fits in the life line of the right palm.

Figure 17
Complete Grip

- The left hand is a combination finger and palm grip. The right hand is mainly a finger grip.
- The hands should feel like a single unit since they must work together.
- Holding the club is a new experience. You may feel and say, "The grip is not comfortable." You would be correct to say the grip is new and different. Do not sacrifice developing the correct grip for what seems "comfortable" to you. It does not follow, however, that the grip should feel awkward and difficult—it is new and will not feel as easy as holding a pencil.
- The grip is for control, touch, and speed. Do not be misled by a feeling of not having a "good hold" on the club. A vise-like, tight grip makes swinging the club impossible. Holding the club with authority is necessary, but this authority is for swinging the club, not for crushing the shaft! Hold the club with the fingers and hands. Do not tense up other body parts as you grip the club.
- The grip should remain the same throughout the swing. Avoid any tendency to release the hold on the club with the last three fingers of the left hand.
- Be careful that you do not wear blisters on your hands. Wearing a glove either on the left hand or on both hands will provide some protection.

The position of the hands on the club affects the directional flight of the ball. For instance, if the right hand is placed on the club so the palm points skyward, the ball is likely to travel to the left of the target. The reason for this can be easily demonstrated. Grip the club with the right hand with the palm facing skyward and the club face square to the intended target. Keeping a firm grip, move the right hand over so the palm faces the intended line of ball flight. Note that the club face turns over and is in a closed position pointing to the left and downward. If either or both hands are placed on the club contrary to the natural hanging position, there will be a tendency for the hand or hands to return to the natural position during the swing, thereby changing the face of the club.

Hand position will not always determine the directional flight of the ball because various compensations and efforts may be made during the swing to affect the club face.

When your game has developed so you have a fairly consistent stroke, you may at times wish to curve the ball to the right or left. A change in the grip may accomplish this for you. Changing the grip from the correct to the incorrect is not recommended for eliminating errors in ball flight.

The Stance

Types of Stance—The usual way of classifying various stances is to draw a relationship between the line on which the feet are placed and the intended line of flight. In the square stance the feet are placed on a line parallel with the intended line of flight. This stance is the most widely used one. It is the most natural position to assume to strike the ball. Any great deviation from this square stance is a point of style or an idiosyncracy. Imitation of such a stance has no merit. If the stance is changed from the square position to an open or closed stance for certain shots, then the change should be slight. A square stance can be recommended for almost all golf shots.

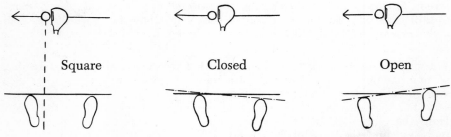

Square   Closed   Open

Figure 18 —Types of Stance

Stances vary in width for a logical reason—the width of the stance should fit the purpose of the swing. If you wish to hit a ball the maximum distance, your feet are placed as far apart as your shoulders are wide. This stance will allow you to swing the club in a wide arc and to keep your balance while swinging the clubhead swiftly. If you wish to hit the ball a short distance you will swing the club in a small, controlled arc, and a narrow stance fits this purpose best. The same principle applies to the distance you stand from the ball. For distance shots, using the longer shafted clubs, you will necessarily stand farther from the ball than you will for the shorter distance shots.

Taking the Stance (See Chapters 5 and 6)

1. Aiming (Step 1, Figures 19 and 20)

   Visualize the shot you desire. Sight to the target. Draw an imaginary line through the ball to the target.

   Holding the club correctly, place the club sole flat on the ground back of the ball. The club face points to the intended target. The edge of the clubhead where the sole and face meet should be perpendicular to the intended line of flight.

2. Placing the Feet (Step 2, Figures 19 and 20)

   For a short approach shot, move your feet to a comfortable narrow stance.

   An open stance may be preferred for this shot.

   For a wood shot, move your feet out to each side to a comfortable stance of approximately shoulder width.

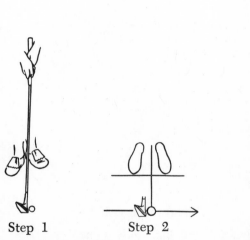

Step 1   Step 2

Figure 19—Taking Stance for Short Approach Shot

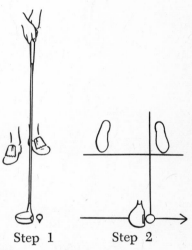

Step 1   Step 2

Figure 20—Taking Stance for Wood Shot

- If the clubhead is placed approximately opposite the center of the stance, the ball will be on a line from a point opposite the inside of the left heel extending toward a point opposite the center of the stance. This is an ideal position for striking most golf shots. (See Figure 21)

- The action of first placing the clubhead back of the ball with the arms easily extended gives you a gauge for the distance you should stand away from the ball. If the feet are positioned first you may have to do considerable shifting back and forth to get the correct distance from the ball.

- For ease and comfort the toes should be turned out slightly and the weight should be about evenly distributed between the feet. The knees are slightly bent. This "give" of the knees is for comfort and readiness to swing the club.

● The body is bent forward from the hip joints and the back is fairly straight, but not rigid. Avoid slumping and rounding the shoulders.

● The arms should be free of the body and "feel" as though they are hanging from the shoulders. In this "'hanging" position the arms will be naturally straight. Trying to hold the arms straight or "stiff" can be a hindrance to learning or performing the golf swing.

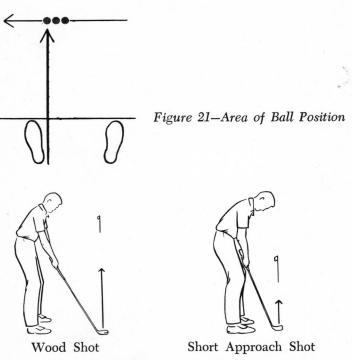

Figure 21—Area of Ball Position

Wood Shot   Short Approach Shot

Figure 22—Addressing the Ball—Side View

The Waggle and Forward Press—A waggle is a movement of the clubhead in preparation to swinging the club. It may be considered a rehearsal for the start of the back swing. After the stance is taken the clubhead is moved away a short distance from the ball in the path in which you intend to swing the club. Then it is moved forward to the ball or up over the ball and back to the address position. This gives you a "feel" of the club and a feeling of ease and confidence for starting the swing. The action of picking the club up and setting it down is not a waggle. Such nervous actions should be avoided. The waggle is not a necessary motion but rather an auxiliary one. As you progress in golf, you will develop a personal style for waggling the club.

A forward press is a movement of the body in preparation to starting the swing. It may be a subtle motion. Just before the swing is started there is a *slight* "give" of the right knee toward the left, thus the name of the action—a press forward. There is no exactness to this movement. Some fine players do not use a forward press. For some beginners a forward press may be a natural movement to make; for others it may be an awkward motion to attempt. If the forward press is not an easy, natural motion, it can best be postponed to a time when the player has more experience in swinging the club.

Practice Suggestions

- Place your hands on the club, check the grip, and release the hold on the club. Practice taking the grip. Do not try to maintain what you think is the correct grip because you fear you will not get this correct grip again.
- A grip maintained for a period of time will become incorrect because of unconscious shifting of the hands and increased tension. The check points of the grip are simple to apply. If these are used you can be confident you will take a correct hold on the club.

- Try taking hold of the club with both hands simultaneously. Have a feeling of the two hands working together and fitting together on the club. This practice will follow that in which you carefully put each hand on the club.

- Holding the club correctly, practice moving the clubhead in the air in various patterns. Write your name with the clubhead, draw circles with the clubhead, etc. Learn to feel control of the clubhead. (See Figure 23)

- Do exercises to develop grip and arm strength. Squeeze a sponge ball or a towel. Flex and extend the fingers and arms offering your own resistance to the movements. Plan a sensible exercise program that will increase your fitness for golf.

- Address the ball and check the address position. As you do so "let go" especially through the shoulders so you will be relaxed and ready to move. Maintain a correct and firm grip.

- Practice taking the stance to different targets. You can check to see if the stance is square by laying a club on the ground with the shaft touching the front tips of your shoes. Then step back of the ball and see if the club shaft is parallel with the intended line of flight. (See Figure 24)

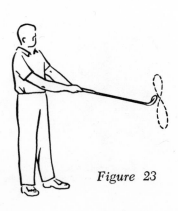

Figure 23

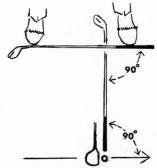

Figure 24—Checking Alignment with Golf Clubs

● Without holding a club, assume an easy, comfortable stance. Check: feet shoulder width apart, body bent forward from the hip joints, knees "easy," and arms hanging free of body. Swing arms a short distance back and forth. Watch a spot on the ground to maintain a steady head position. Let the body and legs "give" with the swing. (See Chapters 5 and 6) Increase the arm swing to a point where one shoulder easily moves under the chin on the backswing and the opposite shoulder moves under the chin on the forward swing. This exercise is excellent for "warm-up" and for learning and registering the "feeling" of the free swinging of the arms and the correct "body posture in motion."

● Make the steps in addressing the ball simple and concise. After you have had some practice in taking the stance avoid making a "production" of it. Place some trust in yourself to aim and to settle in a stance which is good for you.

LEE TREVINO

Pictures by Irv Schloss. Courtesy of Faultless Golf Products, Division of Abbott Laboratories.

Short Approach Shots 5

Approach shots to the putting green played with less than the full swing are pitch shots and chip or run-up shots. In a pitch shot the ball travels in a high trajectory and upon landing tends to stop with little or no roll forward. When a ball is contacted squarely with the high lofted irons, the club face will compress the ball well below its center of gravity, thus imparting backspin to the ball. This backspin and the height from which the ball falls to the ground will tend to stop the forward motion of the ball when it lands. In some instances these two factors will cause the ball to bounce backwards.

In a chip or run-up shot the ball travels in a relatively low trajectory and upon landing tends to roll forward some distance. The medium lofted irons are usually used to hit the run-up shots. The lack of backspin and the low flight of the ball cause the ball to roll forward upon landing.

When swung properly clubs produce the different trajectories of ball flight. The player has only one swing to learn. This swing may be varied in circumference or length.

Approach Situations and Club Selection

In certain approach situations there is little or no choice in the shot you must play. In situation A, Figure 25, you must hit over a deep bunker, land the ball on the green, and have it stay there . . . use a high lofted iron and hit a pitch shot. In situation B, you must strike the ball so it will travel low under the limbs of a tree . . . use an iron with little loft and play a chip shot. In situation C, Figure 26, the area of green to which you must play the ball is small and the green slopes downhill . . . hit a run-up shot into the bank of the hill so that the ball will bounce off the bank onto the green.

When there is a choice in the shot you can play, consider:
1. *Your skill.* Use the club in which you have confidence and success. When practical to do so, choose the chip shot over the pitch shot. First, it is an easier shot for most golfers. Second, if an error such as topping or half-topping is made, the error in shot result is likely to be less with the chip shot. For a given distance a pitch shot must

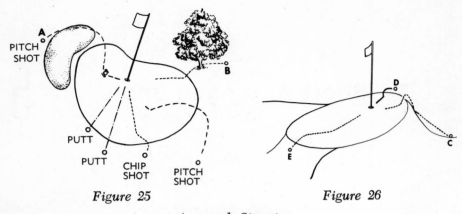

Figure 25   Figure 26

Approach Situations

be struck with greater force than a chip shot. Thus, the pitch shot erroneously hit above center is likely to roll far past the hole and putting green.

2. *The condition of the course.* If the putting surface is dried out and hard, pitch shots will not "hold" on the green. Use run-up shots under these conditions. Ordinarily, do not use chip shots when the ground is very wet and soft.

3. *The contour of the green.* In the approach shot, allow for the ball rolling more when it lands on a downhill surface and rolling less when it lands on an uphill surface. In situation D, Figure 26, the surface is downhill and the hole is close to the edge of the green. Usually an iron with loft would be used to counteract the tendency of the ball to roll downhill. In situation E, a medium iron would be used for a run-up shot.

4. *The lie of the ball.* If the ball is lying on thin turf or on bare ground, it usually is easier to strike the ball effectively with a medium iron than with a high lofted iron.

The Swings

There is no exactness in the length of the swings smaller than the full swing. You must learn to judge how far to swing the club in order to strike the ball a certain distance. You learn to take what you "feel" to be the correct swing for a given distance. No one can tell you the exact swing to take. You learn that through practice. The terms one-quarter, one-half, and three-quarter are sometimes used to describe the approximate lengths of swings. (The three-quarter swing is discussed in the chapter on the full strokes.)

Figure 27—Approximate Quarter Swing

The Quarter Swing

Addressing the Ball

- Take a square stance or a slightly open stance.
- Grip down on the handle of the club.
- Play the ball from an area extending from a point opposite the inside of the left heel to the center of the stance.

Backswing

- Swing the clubhead back close to the ground.
- Watch a spot on the back of the ball where you intend to strike it.
- Concentrate on swinging the clubhead with a feeling of control in the hands.

Swing Through

- Swing the clubhead close to the grass through the ball.
- The ball will be in the way of the club face. Do not make a special effort to meet or hit the ball.
- Try to watch the club face strike the ball.

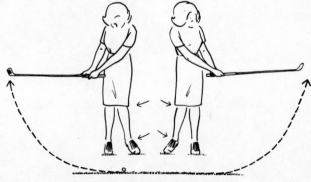

Figure 28—Half Swing

The Half Swing

Backswing

- This longer approach swing is a continuation of the smaller swing.
- The intention and thought is to swing the clubhead away from the ball and distant target, and then toward the ball and the distant target. The clubhead will naturally swing inside the intended line of ball flight and up from the ground.

Swing Through

- The club swings through close to the grass.
- *After the ball is struck,* allow your head to turn naturally to see the shot result.
- The whole swing feels smooth and continuous. The clubhead naturally gains momentum through the contact area.

These swings should not be difficult to learn. They are simple, uncomplicated movements. The details of motion are the *result* of having the correct grip and stance and swinging the clubhead.

- The clubhead is swung in a wide arc keeping the same radius of the swing. *Result*—the left arm will maintain the easy extended position it assumed in addressing the ball.
- During the swing there is a lack of tension in the shoulders and arms. *Result*—there is a free arm and shoulder motion in the swing.
- The grip is correct and firm but not tense. *Result*—there will be a gradual bending of the wrists if the clubhead is swung. If the handle of the club is *carried* back and forth or if it is lifted, there can be no natural responsive action of the wrists. The cooperative action of the wrists becomes more apparent as the swing lengthens. Wrist action is a very gradual motion. It does not occur at a certain spot in the swing. There is no conscious effort to "use" the wrists.

Courtesy of A. G. Spalding & Bros, Inc.

MARILYNN SMITH

● The stance is comfortable and there is a slight bend to the knees. *Result—* there may be a slight give of the body to the direction of the swing—but not a "give" of the head. As you swing back the left knee will naturally give to the right side. There will be a tendency for a slight weight shift to the right foot. As you swing through the opposite action occurs. Like the wrist motion, this action of the body and legs becomes greater and more evident as the swing lengthens.

No one detail of action takes place by itself. There is a *fusion* of all details into a unit of motion. A smooth swing is the result. The swing is efficient. *Only the movement necessary to accomplish the purpose of the swing is made.* There is less movement of the body and its parts in the small swings. As the swing increases in length the movement increases proportionately to produce and accommodate the motion. You can *allow* most of the correct movements—good form—to develop as a result of swinging the clubhead.

Stroke Execution—Some Analysis and Detail

Grip, Hand Action and Wrist Action

If the grip is changed during the swing, an awkward action in the hands and wrists is almost certain to occur. You can check your swing at any point to see if your grip has remained correct. The check is exactly the same as the one used in the address position. Stop your swing at the point where you wish to check it, move your head so that you are looking at your grip, just as you did in the address position, and apply the check points to the grip. In this checking do not move your head until you stop the swing. Suppose you wish to check your grip at the end of the back-swing. Take the correct grip, address the ball properly, and swing the club back and stop. Hold this position. Turn your head to the side so it is in the same *relative* position to your hands as at the address. Now check the grip. The grip should be the same on the club handle as at the address.

A common fault in making the swing for short approach shots is to attempt to scoop the ball up into the air. In this erroneous action, the hands work in opposition to each other in the contact area. The right hand moves forward and under, as the left hand holds back. Through the vital impact area hands *must* move with the club. At times there may even be a feeling of the hands leading the club. If you find that you are striking the ground with the clubhead before you strike the ball, you can suspect that you are trying to scoop the ball. If you will *let* the clubhead do the work for which it was designed, and not try to loft the ball, you can avoid this error.

You can easily check and rehearse the wrist action that occurs in the swing. Keeping the arms extended as in the address position, raise the clubhead and point it forward. As a result of moving the clubhead the wrists will bend. Note that if you lift the handle with the arms there will be no bending of the wrists. (See Figure 29)

Knee Action and Foot Action

Action of the knees, feet and legs is a part of swinging the clubhead in a certain direction. Because of previously developed muscle and tension

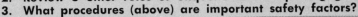

ETIQUETTE ON THE PUTTING GREEN
1. **What 5 points of courtesy are illustrated in the drawing?**
2. **Review 5 other rules of etiquette for the putting green.**
3. **What procedures (above) are important safety factors?**

habits there might be a lack of response in developing this combined action. Rather than complicating the swing by thinking of how to move your feet or which foot to move, this part of the swing can be practiced by itself without breaking up the blending action of all parts of the swing. A simple practice exercise is to alternate bending the left knee toward a spot in front of the right foot, and then bending the other knee so it points to a spot in front of the opposite foot. Accompanying this knee bending is some inward action of the ankle and foot. The weight shifts to the inner border of the foot and big toe. The heel may stay on the ground or raise slightly. When you have trained your muscles to move in this manner and have developed a "feel" for the motion, then you can expect to get the correct action of legs and feet when you swing the club. This practice exercise plus the directional influence of the swing will help develop a natural, unified, correct action. Confusion and complication result if you try to make this action come about by "willing" your knees, legs, and feet to move during a swing.

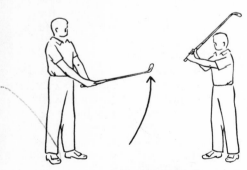

Figure 29—
Wrist Action Exercise

Figure 30—
Foot and Leg Action Exercise

Head Position

In all golf swings the head remains in a fairly stationary position until after the ball is struck. After you contact the ball, your head will turn naturally as it moves to accommodate the follow-through of the swing. There should be no question about this correct mechanical aspect of the swing. The cue "watch the ball until you strike it" accomplishes the steady head position for most people. The cue "keep your head down" can result in serious errors if the idea is overemphasized. If one were to keep his head down so that his chin is resting on his chest, it would be impossible to make a good golf swing. As the body turns during the swing the shoulder moves under the chin. The "head down" position tends to block what would be the natural movement of the shoulders and body. One other serious error that may result from exaggerating this cue is moving the head down and lower during the backswing. This binds the backswing. Then, because the head must be moved back up into the address position to strike the ball, the control and the momentum of the clubhead are destroyed. Until after impact your head should remain still and in the position it is in at the address. However, you should not hold yourself rigid; neither should you concentrate solely on the position of your head.

Practice Suggestions

● Practice swinging all you can. Swing the clubhead back and forth in a pendulum manner, cutting and sweeping the grass with each back and forth movement. When you practice swinging continuously, the speed of the clubhead will be the same for both the backswing and the swing through. This does not happen in a single swing, because the clubhead accelerates through the impact zone. When you take one swing at a time, watch the clubhead sweep the grass then hold the finish of your swing momentarily, feeling control of the club with your hands.

● Hit many chip shots from near the green. Practice until you are machine-like in performance so that there need be no thought regarding the execution of the shot. Aim to roll the ball into the cup, and if the ball does not drop into the cup, have it come to rest very close to the hole. You may find it helpful to pick out a spot on the green where you wish to have the ball land.

● Work from short approaches to longer ones. Change your target both for distance and line of direction. Learn to aim and judge distance. Make mental notes on the different length shots, i.e., how much to "choke up" on the grip, the width of the stance, the necessary length of swing.

● Practice both chip shots and pitch shots. The wedge is the club for the experienced player. Postpone practice with the wedge until you have developed some real skill with the other short irons.

● Practice stroking the ball from good lies on the turf. When you increase your skill, try stroking the ball from good and poor lies. Stroking the ball from other than a good lie is not so much a matter of learning how to do it but rather a matter of facing the situation without anxiety. Practice from various lies, but do not continue practice from poor lies if you are not having success. Such practice tends to destroy confidence and disrupt a good swing pattern.

● Short strokes are an important part of your game. Do not neglect them. Spend the first part of every practice session on these shots.

TOMMY JACOBS

Courtesy of Wilson Sporting Goods Co.

The Full Strokes—
Irons and Woods

6

There is no difference in the way you swing the wood club and the full iron. The swings may feel different to you. This is reasonable for there is a difference in shaft lengths, club balances, club weights, the speed of the swings, and the arc of the swings. In the wood swing the path of the clubhead is closer and more level to the ground for a longer distance through the contact area than it is with the irons. The wood swing may feel more like a sweep than the swing with the irons. One often hears that in playing an iron there should be a feeling of hitting down on the ball. If exaggerated, this cue can lead to great trouble. The swing through the contact area should be one of hitting the ball toward a distant target. The experienced golfer can try hitting down and because of his experience in handling a club, he may not encounter difficulty. For the novice who is trying to learn the swing, this idea of "hitting down" may result in a poor swing and a poor shot. The best idea for most players is to *hit the ball out toward the target*. The swing may feel downward, but do not try to force such an action.

The Irons

Distances and Club Selection—You will learn through practice how far you can hit with each iron. Until you gain some experience there probably will be little difference in the distance you can stroke the ball with the various clubs. You may get greater distance with the medium irons than you do with the long irons. This should not concern you. After hitting many practice shots, you will learn to time your swing correctly for the different lengths of clubs, thus hitting the ball the optimum distance with each club. Until your game develops to the point where there is a consistent difference in the distance you stroke the ball with the various clubs, a minimum set of clubs will probably serve you best.

The irons are versatile clubs. You can hit the ball from various situations with them. You can make certain adjustments to vary the distances and trajectories of ball flight. For instance, the shot you wish to make is too far for a #7 iron, and a #5 iron will be too much club for the distance. You do not have a #6 iron. Do not try to extend the distance you normally can hit with the #7 iron. Take a #5 iron, either grip down on the leather or take a shorter swing or do both. Keep the same tempo in the swing as you would in making any golf stroke. Do not purposely slow down the swing.

If you wish to hit the ball in a higher or lower trajectory than normal for a club, you change the angle of the club face when you address the ball. Increasing the club face angle to get more loft to the shot is called "opening the face," and decreasing the angle is called "closing the face."

Playing the High Lofted Irons—When you use the high lofted irons, #7 and above, you have a short club designed for a high degree of accuracy. A swing somewhat less than the full swing is recommended for these shots. This is sensible for there is less movement involved in a three-quarter swing than a full swing, thus a greater chance of being accurate. This motion is an extension of the half swing. No great effort need be made to increase the swing. With a purpose of stroking the ball a slightly longer distance, you will naturally take a longer swing. Some fine players use an approximate three-quarter swing for all the full iron shots and for the wood shots.

Figure 31—The Three-Quarter Swing

The Woods

Club Selection—When you play golf on a regulation course you probably will tee off with a wood on at least 14 of the 18 holes. Most courses have four par 3 holes. All or some of the par 3 holes will be less than wood length. On many of the long holes your drive from the tee will be followed by using a wood if the lie of the ball and the distance warrant it. Hitting long, straight wood shots is surely one of the great pleasures of golf. It is pleasant to see the ball travel this long distance, and it is a great feeling to coordinate this complex movement so that the maximum clubhead speed and accuracy are attained at contact and through the contact area. In a fine wood shot the club is literally flying through the impact zone. It is important to note this. You trust that the swiftly moving clubhead will stroke the ball squarely.

Due to the size and shape of the clubhead and the little loft of the club face, the woods are not as versatile clubs as the irons. The driver is designed to strike the ball from a tee. Only in rare circumstances would it be used from the fairway. The lie of the ball is a more important factor than the distance in deciding whether you will use a wood and what wood you will use. Even though you are a wood distance from the green, the circumstances under which you must play the ball may necessitate your

PLAYING SITUATIONS—Hole #8

Study each situation, 0-9, then plan the best way to play the shot.
(You have the minimum set of 7 clubs recommended in the text)
1. Estimate the distance to the hole.
2. Determine and visualize the shot you desire.
3. Decide on the best club for the shot.
4. Are there particulars unique to the situation?
Imagine your ball in other positions and plan your strategy of play.

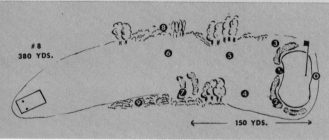

#8
380 YDS.

←——— 150 YDS. ———→

using an iron rather than a wood. The #2 wood can be used only from an exceptionally good lie on the fairway. The higher lofted woods, #4 and #5, can be used for poorer lies and shorter distances than the #2 and #3 woods. If you have only one wood in your starting set, choose the #3 wood because you can use it on the tee and from the fairway.

Distance and the Correct Purpose—Progressing to stroking the ball with the woods should not be a complicated step if your objective is to strike the ball to a target farther away but within your distance potential. If the objective should become hitting the ball with all one's might, complications arise: poor coordinations and muscle tensions. They are the curse of the beginner and experienced player alike.

You do not have to know muscle action to make a golf swing, but some practical knowledge about muscle action can be helpful to you. Try this experiment related to using muscles effectively and ineffectively. Extend your right arm out in front of you with your palm facing up. Bend the right elbow and touch your fingers to your shoulder. Return the arm to your side. Now extend your arm out similarly again but this time tightly tense (contract) all the muscles of your arm. Keeping the muscles tense, try bending your elbow. This action is now difficult, if not impossible. Why? You are preventing muscles used in the motion to perform. When you relax—let go—they can perform. Tensing up as you want the arm to move is like stepping on your car's accelerator and brake at the same time.

If you try to hit the ball "hard" as far or even farther than you can, you tend to use muscles in such a way that they resist and even "block" the intended movement. This great exertion of tensing up muscles gives you the *false feeling* that this is the way to accomplish the goal of hitting the ball a long distance.

Muscular contractions of resistance plus the strong muscular contractions to overcome the resistance may make you feel more powerful, but they spell ruin for distance and accuracy of a golf stroke. As a novice or an experienced player, you can be easily misled by the "feeling" of a golf swing. When you hit a fine shot a considerable distance you are apt to think or say: "I swung so easy." That is true. You did swing easy "muscle-wise." The muscle action was synchronized. Resistant muscular contractions were avoided, and the right muscular contractions were made so the swing felt "good." After such an experience you may think: "If I can hit the ball that far swinging 'easy,' then I'll put something into the swing and really hit the ball farther." This theorizing may seem logical. But what will you put into the swing? If it is more clubhead speed, then you can expect a longer shot. If you are misled by the feeling of "muscling the ball," then you probably can expect to hit the ball a shorter distance. When the swing felt "easy," you may have been swinging with the greatest clubhead speed.

No one can tell you the correct amount or kind of muscle action and relaxation that you should have in your swing. The fine synchronization of muscle contraction and relaxation occurring throughout the golf swing is beyond human description, but this synchronization is within human achievement.

The Swing

Addressing the Ball

1. Aim to a definite target. Be certain the target is within your distance potential.
2. Assume a comfortable position with a feeling of readiness to swing.
3. Your feet should be approximately shoulder width apart. The stance may be slightly wider for the woods than for the irons.
4. If a waggle is made in preparation for the swing, move the clubhead back low to the ground as you would in the start of the backswing.

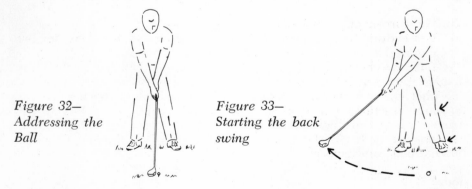

Figure 32—
Addressing the
Ball

Figure 33—
Starting the back
swing

Starting the Swing

1. The club is swung back close to the ground.
2. There is a natural give of the body and legs in the direction of the swing. The head remains in the same position as at address.
3. The feeling and effort is one of swinging the clubhead straight back away from the ball. When the clubhead reaches a certain point it will naturally swing inside the intended line of flight.

4. The feeling of starting the clubhead away from the ball should be one of ease. Do not hurry the start, lift, or "grab" the club handle to start the swing.

Top of the Swing

1. The club is swung back to a position in which the shaft is approximately horizontal.
2. The left arm remains easily extended.
3. The right elbow is pointing down and comfortably, but slightly, away from the side. Trying to keep the elbow against the side binds the swing and reduces the size of the arc.
4. The wrists are bent (cocked) so they are approximately under the shaft.

Figure 34—
Top of the Swing—Front View

Figure 35—
Top of the Swing—Side View

5. The correct grip has been maintained.
6. The body is turned so that you are looking at the ball over the left shoulder.
7. Some weight has been shifted to the right foot. For most golfers the left heel will be raised slightly to accommodate the body turn.
8. The hips and shoulders have turned. The body has maintained the same position in relation to the ball as at address. The body has turned or coiled, but it has not moved sideways.
9. The arc of the backswing was naturally and simultaneously around the body and upward.

The Downswing

1. As the swing changes direction, there should be no rush into the downswing. The swing should feel like a continuous motion, even though there is a change of direction.
2. The purpose of taking the long backswing was to get the clubhead a distance away from the ball so it can gradually accelerate in the downswing and reach its maximum speed at contact.
3. The downswing is a natural motion of "getting set" to contact the ball with a swiftly moving clubhead.

4. As a result of "getting set" and reserving the greatest clubhead speed for impact, certain actions can be noted:

● The left heel returns to its original position on the ground and the weight begins to shift to the left side.

● The arms swing downward with the left arm remaining in its extended position and the right elbow coming into the side.

● The wrists remain in a cocked position reserving the action of the clubhead for later in the swing.

● The body uncoils, turns in the direction of the swing.

● These actions blend one into the other. They take their places as parts of the downswing.

5. In striking a golf ball you do *not TRY* to do the analysis described. These actions will occur naturally with a correct purpose in swinging the club, and with practice.

Figure 36—
Downswing—Front View

Figure 37—
Downswing—Side View

Impact

1. The body is in a firm position of balance to allow the clubhead to reach its maximum speed.

2. The clubhead catches up with the hands. There is no "wrist snap" in that the clubhead passes the hands. The hands continue moving with the clubhead through the contact area.

3. Concentrate on striking the ball to a target.

4. The head remains still. It is impossible to see the clubhead strike the ball, but the idea of "watching the club strike the ball" is a good one to follow.

Follow-through

1. The clubhead swings through close to the ground. No attempt is made to hit the ball into the air.

Figure 38—Impact—Front View   *Figure 39—Contact—Side View*

2. The purpose of the swing is to hit the ball to a distant target. This purpose and the clubhead speed determine the proper follow-through. If the purpose is only to "hit" the ball, the chances are poor that the follow-through will be correct. You do not "will" a fancy formful follow-through. It is a result.

3. Good balance has been maintained throughout the swing.

4. The clubhead speed with its resultant centrifugal force exerts an outward pull reacting on the arms, body, and legs.

5. At the finish of the swing, the hips have turned along with the shoulders so you are facing the intended target. The head turns to accommodate the full finish of the swing and to see the shot result.

6. The right knee has bent and turned so it is touching or almost touching the left knee.

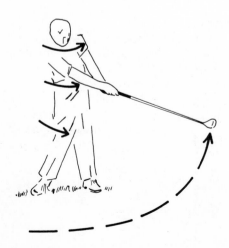 

Figure 40—Follow-through

Figure 41—Follow-through Completed

Practice Suggestions

● Start practice sessions with the short iron strokes and work to the full swings with the irons and woods.

● As you practice, note the length of the shots. Learn distances as you practice. For instance, learn to hit the ball 75 yards, 100 yards, 130 yards, etc. This will prepare you for playing golf.

● As you take practice swings without hitting a ball, watch the club cut through the grass. Work for a smooth, swift swing. If you wish to check the position of your head when you swing, stand so your shadow casts in front of you and watch the shadow of your head.

● If you have difficulty with the long irons and woods, try gripping down on the handle of the club. This shorter hold on the club may give you more control and successful shots.

● If you are having trouble with the long shots off the grass—the woods and the irons—then tee the ball and hit some shots. After you have had some success hitting the ball from a tee, then place the ball in a good lie on the turf and practice hitting off the grass. Do not fear making the stroke easier by teeing the ball. When you are hitting your shots well, then you can try hitting the ball from various positions on the turf.

● Practice hitting all shots to a specific target. This gives your swing the correct purpose.

● Practice the exercises for the footwork and the body turn.

● Practice swinging the club as if it were a baseball bat. Take the golf grip and let the left arm remain easily extended during the swing. Swing the club over your right shoulder, then over your left shoulder. Through the contact area swing the club at shoulder height, waist height, and then close to the ground like the golf swing.

● As you practice to increase the distance of your stroke, do not tighten up. Do the opposite, loosen up.

● At times overextend yourself in practice to develop endurance of a physical and mental (concentration) nature. After a good practice session you may well be tired. Any golfer with a low handicap knows the work involved in developing a golf game. This is one of the pleasures of golf.

Figure 42—Exercise for the Body Turn

SAM SNEAD

Courtesy of Wilson Sporting Goods Co.

7 The Putting Stroke

The variety of clubs used for putting is an indication of the individuality in the putting stroke. There is no one style of putter that can be recommended for successful strokes. Some golfers use one putter throughout their golfing years. They would not consider changing putters even though they change woods and irons as new models are marketed. At the other extreme are the golfers who blame the club for all their putting woes and change putters frequently. Generally they never find the right putter.

Individuality is also asserted by golfers in the choice of the grip and stance for putting. Various styles of grip and stance are used. Comfort and ease, rather than rules of position, are key factors in taking the grip and stance. There is general agreement on certain principles to be followed. It is recommended that you adopt a style of grip and stance that would follow these principles.

The Grip

- The reverse overlapping grip is the most widely used.
- In this grip, the index finger of the left hand either overlaps the little finger of the right hand or extends down overlapping more than one finger.
- The thumbs are straight down the front of the shaft.
- The palms may either oppose each other or assume a more "open" position than they do in the conventional grips for the woods and irons.
- The club is held with an ease and a touch for executing a delicate stroke.
- The club may be held at its full length or slightly less than full length. An extremely short hold on the club is not recommended because of the long distance the club would have to be swung for long putts.

The Stance

- The width of the stance may vary from a wide stance to a very narrow one. A medium width, comfortable stance is recommended.
- The sole of the club is placed flat on the putting surface back of the ball. With the club in this position you will naturally stand close to the ball, with your arms close to your body, and your eyes directly above the ball.
- The elbows may be easily bent. For steadiness in making the stroke, the right forearm can be placed against the right thigh.

● The ball may be played in any position from a point in front of the left
foot to a point out from the center of
the stance. If the ball is played opposite the left foot, there may be a natural
shift of the weight to the left foot in
addressing the ball.

● The knees are easily bent.

The Swing

The putter head is swung back and
forth close to the ground in a pendular-
like motion. Naturally the length of the
swing will vary with the distance of the
putt. On short putts the putter will
swing back and through on the intended
line of roll. On long putts your feeling
should be one of swinging the putter

Figure 43—Putting Stance

on the line, but the putter head will naturally swing in on the backswing
and the follow-through. The movement is a combination of hand, wrist,
and arm action. The body should remain still. It has no contribution to
make to this small swing, except stability. Ease is the key to good putting.
During the swing and especially the follow-through there should be a
feeling of the hands moving with the putter head. The ball should not
be jabbed with the putter head while the hands are held back. Like all
strokes, watch the putter stroke the ball.

Aiming

To aim correctly you simply have the face of the club pointing to
your objective. Your objective may be the hole or may be a spot on the
green if you have to allow for a down and sidehill roll of the ball. When
you address the ball, be certain it is lined up with the center of the club
face, never toward the toe of the club. It may be helpful to momentarily
place the putter head in front of the ball to line up the face with the
objective. In the address position turn your head to the objective while
you sight and visualize the desired putt, then run your eyes back along
the line through the ball and beyond it where you intend to start the
putter back. Proceed to stroke the ball without unnecessary delay. Delay
tends to induce tension.

Your objective in putting should be to roll the ball into the cup, but
if the ball does not drop into the hole then you want it to come to rest
inches or less from the hole. The adage "never up, never in" is a good
one to remember. Put the ball as far as the hole, then it will have a
chance to drop in the cup.

Judgment Factors

In addition to judging distances to stroke the ball, you have other
judgments to make. You must figure how to play a slope or undulation.

You must learn to judge how easily the ball will roll over the putting surface. This is called "reading" a green. As you wait your turn to putt, try to stand near your ball, preferably in back of it. (See rules of etiquette.) When your turn comes to putt, you have already studied your line and figured any "break" (contour) of the green. As you wait, also learn from watching other putts. If you have a sidehill putt, and another player has already played a similar stroke, then you have the best information you can get for playing your stroke.

Putting greens are referred to as "fast" or "slow," depending upon how easily the ball rolls over the surface. The condition and type of grass determines how fast or slow a green will be. If the turf is thin and dried out the green will be faster than if the turf is thick and wet. A variety of grasses is used for putting greens. One type of grass is a bent grass. The grain of this grass influences the role of the ball. A putt against the grain will require a firmer stroke and a putt with the grain a lighter stroke. You can make some judgment as to how fast or how slow greens will be by practicing on the practice green before you start your round, and then watching the stroke results of your playing companions during play.

Practice Suggestions

- Use several golf balls and start your practice with the balls about a foot away from the hole. Simply stroke the balls into the cup with little or no thought regarding how it is done. Gradually increase the distance to long putts. Let your "instinct" for aiming and judging take over. If the ball does not fall into the cup, it should come to rest very close to the hole.

- Stroke the ball and listen for it to drop in the cup. This gives you calmness and confidence, not anxiety over the result. The person who starts steering a putt immediately upon stroking the ball has only the intention of missing the putt, not of making it.

- Practice at home on carpeting. It does not matter if the surface is different than grass. You are practicing to develop a stroke and swing.

- When necessary, review some putting fundamentals. After the review, proceed to concentrate on sinking putts.

- After a session of starting with short putts and working back to long distances, try a variety of putts—short, long, uphill, downhill, sidehill, and from off the apron of the green. Practice lining up the putts without delay. Learn to size up the situation and proceed at once to make the putt.

- If in practice (or play) the putts are "rimming" the cup, with many close putts and "just misses," don't fret. You are putting well. The putts will start dropping so don't change this good stroke.

- On sidehill putts visualize the curved path on which the ball must roll to drop into the cup. Pick out a spot on this path for your point of aim—as a bowler might do in spot bowling. Use such points as a different colored section of grass or a dead blade of grass. (A dead blade of grass may be removed, but if it is an aid in aiming, make use of it. It will not deflect the roll of the ball.)

- A good practice session should last at least a half-hour, preferably longer.

● Some of your practice may be in match or stroke competition with another player. This practice is enjoyable, stimulating and challenging; however, your best practice will be done alone. Be determined in your practice. Good putting is up to you.

● Work for a smooth, simple, easy, and comfortable stroke avoiding all unnecessary movement.

Courtesy of Wilson Sporting Goods Co.

BILLY CASPER

8 Shots Requiring Special Consideration

Playing from a Bunker (Sand Trap)

A variety of shots can be played from a bunker. The factors determining what shot should be played are: (1) the lie of the ball in the sand, (2) the physical features of the bunker, and (3) the desired distance of the shot. If the bunker is shallow and the ball is lying in a good position, you will have few or no adjustments to make. If the bunker is a deep one with overhanging turf, or the ball is lying deep in the sand, then you will have to play your shot in a manner different from the usual golf shot.

In playing from a sand trap, you cannot ground the clubhead. You may take a practice swing provided you do NOT touch the sand during the swing. (See Chapter 10, Rules.)

Situation A—Your ball is in a shallow sand trap 200 yards from the green. The ball is lying in a good position on the sand.
1. Choose a club in which you have confidence. Avoid using a wood until you have experience in playing from bunkers. There is a good chance that it will take you two strokes to get on the green, so you can afford to sacrifice some distance in hitting from the trap, and then make up this distance in your next shot from the fairway.
2. When you address the ball, work your feet down into the sand for a firm stance.
3. When you take your stroke, contact the ball before you contact the sand. Swing to strike the ball to a target. Do not try to help get the ball from the trap—the club face loft will do that for you.

Situation B—Your ball is lying in a shallow sand trap adjacent to the putting green. There is no overhanging turf on the bunker. The ball is in a good lie.
1. Either play a short iron to the putting green as you would a short approach shot,
2. Or use the putter and play the shot as you would a putt, rolling the ball out of the sand onto the putting surface. This is an easy shot to play, and it is used successfully by the expert golfer as well as the novice.

Situation C—Your ball is lying in a deep sand trap that has over-hanging turf or deep in a footprint in soft sand. The bunker is adjacent to the putting green. (See Figure 44 and 45.)
1. It is obvious that you must use a club that will loft the ball quickly and sharply to clear the high bank.
2. You may open the face of the club so it points more skyward. If you do not have a wedge, you can open the face of the highest lofted iron you carry and successfully execute the shot.

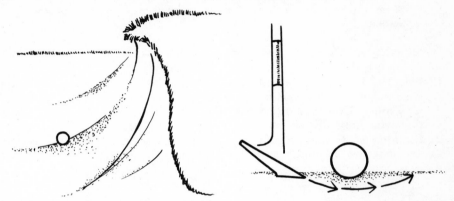

Figure 44—Ball in Deep Bunker   *Figure 45—The "Explosion Shot"*

3. Work your feet into the sand for a firm stance. Play the ball toward the left foot. If desired, an open stance can be taken.
4. Aim to strike the sand one to three inches back of the ball. The texture of the sand and the distance you wish to hit the shot will determine how far back of the ball you strike the sand. The club face does not actually touch the ball. There is a cushion of sand between the club face and the ball. The length of the swing may vary from a short swing to a full swing.
5. This shot is referred to as an "explosion shot." Do not be misled by the term and hit and dig deep into the sand in an explosive manner. Be certain you continue swinging the club through the sand and ball, sweeping out the sand with the ball. The swing should be smooth and continuous, not violent.

Playing Hillside Lies
When you are playing a shot from a very slight, gentle slope assume a comfortable, balanced stance and play the shot just as you would any golf shot. If the hillside is steep, then you may find it necessary to make some adjustments in playing the shot. However, do not become overly technical and complicate your execution of the stroke. For instance, instead of trying to follow detailed pointers on weight distribution, trust your instinctive sense of feel for taking a comfortable stance and maintaining good balance.

WHAT IS THE RULE?

1. A rake lying in a sand trap interferes with play.
2. A ball lies in a runway made by a burrowing animal.
3. For the correct way to drop a ball.
4. A ball comes to rest on the wrong putting green.
5. On the green casual water lies between your ball and the hole; a ball lies in casual water on the fairway.
6. For lost ball; an unplayable ball.
7. A ball lies against an out of bounds fence; against a protective screen.

Situation A—You have a sidehill-uphill lie. You have to stand so one foot is higher than the other. (See Figure 46)

1. Play the ball toward the higher foot. Settle in your stance and get your balance. In addressing the ball, be careful that you do not cause it to move. To avoid this, place the clubhead farther back of the ball than you normally do.
2. On long shots aim slightly to the right of your intended target as you may have a tendency to hit the ball to the left from this position.

Situation B—You have a sidehill-downhill lie. (See Figure 47)

1. Play the ball toward the higher foot.
2. On long shots there may be a tendency to hit to the right so allow for this by aiming to the left of your intended target.
3. If you need loft to the shot, use a club with more loft than you generally would as there will be a tendency for the ball to travel in a lower trajectory than normal.

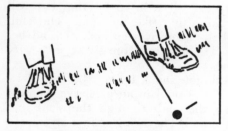   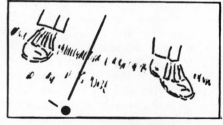

Figure 46—Uphill Lie   *Figure 47—Downhill Lie*

Situation C—Your feet are on level ground; the ball is on a level below your feet.

1. Settle well down in your stance to keep your balance in swinging.
2. There may be a tendency to hit to the right, so aim slightly to the left.

Situation D—Your feet are on level ground, the ball is on a level above your feet.

1. If necessary, grip down on the handle of the club.
2. Aim slightly to the right as there may be a tendency to strike the ball to the left.

Courtesy of Wilson Sporting Goods Co.

JULIUS BOROS

Playing from the Rough

In playing from the rough there is one primary objective—to hit the ball out of the rough into a position where your next shot can be easily played. Be willing to sacrifice distance by playing a safe shot free of the rough.

- If the growth of the rough is high, it is necessary to swing the clubhead in a more upward arc on the backswing to avoid the interference of the tall grass.
- Use a club that will raise the ball sharply into the air.
- Maintain a firm grip on the club and keep swinging the clubhead through the ball. Do not merely chop at the ball.
- In addressing the ball or in moving loose impediments, be careful that you do not cause the ball to move.

Playing in the Wind

Judging how the wind will affect the flight of the ball and playing shots in the wind is one of the interesting and exasperating challenges of golf. To check the direction of the wind, note how the pennant of the flagstick is blowing, or break off some blades of grass and toss them into the air and note which way they fly.

Situation A—The wind is blowing the same direction as the desired shot.

1. If you are teeing off make use of the wind in getting greater distance. Tee the ball higher if using the driver, or use a more lofted wood to drive from the tee.
2. If you are playing an iron to the green, consider if the wind is strong enough to carry your ball a greater distance, thus warranting the use of a shorter iron.
3. Do not try to hit high pitch shots to the putting green. The wind will take the backspin off the ball and you will find yourself well past the green. Play low shots into the green.

Situation B—The wind is blowing the opposite direction of your desired shot.

1. If you are teeing off, tee the ball lower for a possible lower flight to the ball.
2. Figure the wind will decrease the distance of a shot, so select a longer club than you would generally use.
3. Do not try to hit high pitch shots to the putting green. It is too difficult to judge how much the wind will affect the ball flight.
4. There is a tendency to try to swing harder, resulting in poor shots. Do not change your swing in an effort to fight the wind.

Situation C—The wind is blowing across the direction of the desired shot.

1. Aim into the wind to allow for the carry of the ball in the wind direction.
2. In general try to play lower shots that will be less affected by the wind.

Improving Your Golf Game 9

Concentration and the Mental Side

● You can think positively and with confidence about your golf strokes after you have spent enough time in practice to learn to stroke the ball well. Your initial approach to the game must be that you CAN learn it, then this must be followed by much practice. From this you will develop a positive attitude toward each shot you must play. This positive attitude which is necessary for good golf cannot be fantasy. It must be something real, based on experience.

● A round of golf gives you much time to think and to talk. A formula of concentration and correct mental attitude for you to follow in these hours cannot be given. This you must develop. You will learn what is right for you.

● Stroke each shot with the idea that you will accomplish your purpose. Plan your stroke, come to a definite decision, visualize the shot you desire, and then proceed to execute it without delay.

● During a round of golf no instruction about a golf swing should be given. If you are having a bad day, accept it as such. Do not seek advice from another player. Also do not offer to teach someone or give playing tips.

● The only strategy in competition is to play your own game. Players have been known to use schemes to upset their opponents, but this is not golf.

● Accept the responsibility for the shots you play. What someone else says or does should not affect your game adversely. Do not blame anyone for a bad shot. Keep control of your game—then you can improve it.

● If you hit one poor shot or more, do not hastily decide you are "off your game." The result of a poorly hit shot is sometimes satisfactory or even excellent. A few poorly hit shots do not necessarily make a bad round. No doubt you will have some poor shots—but they may be a blessing in disguise—you may make a brilliant recovery from a poor shot, and it will stimulate you to play an excellent round.

● Do not label yourself negatively as "I can't putt," "I can't aim," "I can't use my #3 wood," etc. This ruins your game. Also such statements made verbally are boring and disturbing to your fellow players.

● Enjoy your good golf shots.

● There is no secret to the mental side of golf and no hypnotic spell you can put yourself under to play good golf. Use your own good common sense in working out a plan of concentration.

CORRECTING BALL FLIGHT ERRORS

You top several shots. Another player tells you: "You looked up. Keep your head down." Is this the only or best correction for topping? Consider club face and ball impact, your purpose in striking the ball, and practice methods for eliminating the error.

To correct slicing and hooking the ball consider: What club face and ball impact cause the ball to curve in flight? How might an incorrect grip or stance affect ball flight? What are the check points for the correct grip and stance? Can "extra effort" in the impact zone cause the error?

Corrections

● There are a myriad of theories for hitting golf shots and correcting swings. At any given time you can go to a practice range and get free lessons by asking advice from almost any player. The value of these "free" lessons can be questioned. Many golfers like to tell their "secrets" of success. These tips vary from day to day. A tip that seems a miraculous cure one day is discarded the next day. Do not be hasty in adopting these tips.

● If you are taking golf lessons you must work with your instructor. He sees your golf swing and the shot results. He has experience in teaching and has something to offer. If you are working on pet theories of your own and not following his instructions, then your time and his time are being wasted. Tell your instructor what you have been trying to do in your swing. This will give him a lead in helping you. If you do not understand the instruction, ask questions seeking information, not questions of the contentious type. You may have read what a top playing professional said about the swing and misinterpreted the information. This should be clarified. The top playing professional is a great golfer, and he is sincere in the statements he makes about his golf game, but some of his instructions may be directed to the experienced, low handicap player. These ideas may not be useful to the novice player.

● When you are taking a lesson and the instructor gives you a cue for your swing, do not expect a miracle to happen with the next shot. The result of one shot or a few shots is not absolute proof of the worth or worthlessness of instruction. If you hit a poor shot, do not say or think "See, it doesn't work," or "I can't do it your way."

● After your instructor gives you a cue to change your swing, it may "feel" to you that you are doing what he says and that the swing has changed drastically. The instructor, however, may see no change at all. For example, you have been swinging the club back beyond the position where the shaft is horizontal. The instructor asks you to take a three-quarter swing. You sincerely try to follow instructions and it "feels" as though you have, yet the teacher says you still swung below the horizontal position. The tremendous change of "feel" you experience may not at all match what actually takes place in the swing. Realize that you may "feel" a great difference in your swing, but no change may be obvious to the instructor.

● If you are having trouble with a particular club or shot, do not decide that you will proceed only with correcting and mastering the club or shot. If you are playing good shots in general, then this error is a mental thing of your own making. You actually prevent yourself from performing well by predetermining the outcome. Put the club away or forget it. Work on strokes you are hitting well, then go back to your "problem" for short practice periods.

● If you are hitting a variety of error shots in a practice session do not try to correct each one. Perhaps you have been experimenting with your swing and these shots are the results. Golf can be very frustrating so you make various efforts in the contact area to hit the ball, all producing different shots. Assuming your swing is basically good, do not continue trying various corrections. Hit some short shots. Concentrate on a smooth swing and striking the ball to your target. Gradually work to the longer shots. Do not hesitate to go back to the shorter strokes if you lose your touch again. *Give yourself a chance to regain your swing and your touch for stroking the ball.*

● Topping the ball is a common error. The ball is hit above its center, thus imparting topspin to the ball. A ball struck in this manner may travel in the air a short distance then dive to the ground and roll, or may just roll along the ground. In correcting this error concern yourself with the clubhead and ball contact. The following suggestions should correct topping.

1. Ask yourself, "what am I trying to do?" If you are trying to hit the ball into the air or get under the ball, you have the wrong purpose. This purpose will lead to topping. Try to hit the ball so it will travel low. This will influence you to keep the clubhead low through the contact area.

2. Watch the club face strike the ball. Look at the spot at the "waist" of the back of the ball. Aim to strike the ball at this spot. Do not be anxious about the shot result.

3. If the ball is teed up, sweep out the tee as you strike the ball. If the ball is on the grass, sweep the grass after you strike the ball.

4. Practice swinging without the ball and sweep the clubhead low through the contact area.

5. Do not tense up the shoulders and arms in the contact area, thereby drawing the club in toward you and away from the ball.

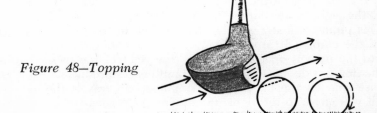

Figure 48—Topping

One obvious result of trying to hit the ball up and swinging the clubhead up is that the body will react to this upward motion. The weight may not shift to the left foot. In extreme cases there may be a shift of weight to the right foot with a raising of the left heel. This strange form is the *result* of the erroneous upward action of the clubhead.

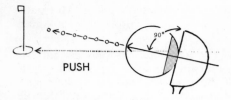

PUSH

PULL—Straight Shot to Left of Target
  - Clubhead Path through Impact is on a Line Toward the Left of the Target—From Outside-In.
  - Club Face is Perpendicular to Clubhead Path.

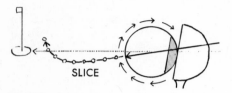

SLICE

HOOK—Ball Curves to Left due to Counter-Clockwise (horizontal) Spin
  - Clubhead Path through Impact can be: 1. On a Line to the Target, 2. From Inside-Out, 3. From Outside-In.
  - Club Face is Pointing to the Left of the Clubhead Path.

PUSH—Straight Shot to Right of Target
  - Clubhead Path through Impact is on a Line Toward the Right of the Target—From Inside-Out.
  - Club Face is Perpendicular to the Clubhead Path.

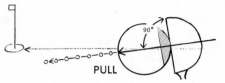

PULL

SLICE—Ball Curves to Right due to Clockwise (horizontal) Spin
  - Clubhead Path through Impact can be: 1. On a Line to the Target, 2. From Outside-In, 3. From Inside-Out.
  - Club Face is Pointing to the Right of the Clubhead Path.

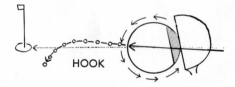

HOOK

Figure 49—Mechanics: Directional Flight of Ball*

- Another common error in striking the ball is hitting to the right of the intended target. A ball that travels on a straight line to the right is a *push* shot; a shot that travels in an arc to the right is called a *slice* or *fade*. In a push shot the path of the clubhead through the contact area is on a line toward the right of the target and the club face is perpendicular to this line. This produces a straight shot but off line to the right. In a slice, the path of the clubhead through contact can vary, but the club face in relation to the path is open or facing to the right of the path. In this contact the inner side of the ball is compressed, producing a horizontal, clockwise spin on the ball. As the spinning ball travels through the air, the ball will curve to the right. In considering corrections for these errors assume that the grip and stance are correct and the golf swing in general appears to be one of good form. There are no unusual or outstanding obvious distortions in swinging the club. If this is true, the error is produced by incorrect efforts in the contact area.

  1. One of the main reasons for hitting to the right is trying to put something extra into the shot. Instead of swinging the club face to the

*See Figure 10—Impact Producing Straight Shot to Target.

square position the handle is pushed, thus changing either the path of the club, the club face, or both. Develop the feeling of swinging the clubhead *through* the contact area. (See Figure 49)

2. Do not be anxious or fearful over the shot result, thereby tending to stop the swing and leaving the club face open.

3. Do not try to get a straight follow-through or "steer" the ball to your target. Trust that the clubhead will travel in the correct path and strike the ball squarely.

4. Do not allow for any error to the right by aiming to the left of your target. You will only become more adept at the error and compound it.

5. If you have been swinging with the club face open at contact, it may "feel" that the club face is closed when you swing it to the square position. Because of this "feel" already established, you may actually have to attempt to swing the face to a closed position to reach the square position. Do not be fearful of trying to do this. If after trying the correction the ball travels straight, then you know that the face was square even if it "felt" closed to you. If the ball travels to the left then an overcorrection was made, thus producing a hook or pull.

The traditional correction for slicing has been to hit "from inside out." This may have some value for the person who has a very distorted swing with the clubhead travelling from way outside and across the intended line of flight. This is not the error of most people. Using only this cue may increase the error of hitting to the right. Recall that the path of the clubhead through the contact area should be from inside the intended line—on the intended line—and then inside again.

A closed stance is suggested frequently to correct slicing. If the player takes a closed stance and has a feeling he is aiming to the right, and then compensates for this aim by swinging the face over to direct the ball to the intended target, a closed stance would be an aid. This does not necessarily happen. Trick shot artists prove that the stance in itself does not determine ball flight. They can take any stance, stand on one foot, or even sit down and hit the ball any direction they please. The path of the clubhead through the impact area and the relation of the club face to this path determines the directional ball flight.

Playing Hints

● Play according to the rules and keep your score accurately. Your objective is to play golf, not a game of chicane.

● Study and know the golf rules. Not knowing the rules may cause you to be penalized strokes, and knowing the privileges of the rules may help you play a better game. One example of a benefit of knowing the rules is: when you are going to drop a ball back of a water hazard, you may choose a nice, grassy area on which to drop the ball, providing all the other provisions of the rule are followed. (See rules—water hazard.)

● Play the course as you find it without complaints about it. You choose the course, it does not choose you.

● When you are teeing off and there is trouble to one side of the fairway, tee your ball to the side where there is trouble, then if you aim toward the center of the fairway you are aiming away from the difficulty.

Who is the only golfer to have won the U.S. Open, U.S. Amateur, British Open, and British Amateur titles in the same year? Who are the present title holders? Name other major tournaments held for men and for women in the U.S. Who are the present title holders?

- In your early games of golf improving the lie of the ball on the fairway may be condoned. After you have developed your game, however, play the ball as it lies on the fairway according to the official U.S.G.A. rules. Continued play of winter rules is not golf and will make your stroking the ball difficult when you are required to play summer rules.

- Do not hesitate to play a safe shot when a daring one may get you into great trouble.

- If you can hit a 5-iron 140 yards and another player in your group uses a 7-iron for this shot, do not be challenged into trying to hit your 7-iron 140 yards. Your objective is to score well, not to hit an iron a particular distance.

- When you play golf choose the correct club for a shot by considering:

  1. The *lie* of the ball on the ground.
  2. The *situation,* such as do you have to hit the ball in a high or low trajectory, etc.
  3. The *distance* you want to strike the ball.
  4. The *course conditions,* such as how is the wind blowing? is the turf wet and soft or is it dried out? etc.
  5. What is *your skill* with the different clubs? Choose a club in which you have confidence and success.

- When the lie of the ball is a poor one, for example, on thin, sparse grass or on bare ground, take a practice swing over a spot similar in nature (if such a spot is near your ball). You have then faced the situation and are less apt to be concerned about hitting from the poor lie.

- To avoid tension, don't over-respond to a situation. For instance, you see your ball roll into a distant sand trap. Do not immediately react in fear and anxiety over playing the next shot. Discipline yourself in thought control. When you reach the sand trap, size up the situation, plan the shot, and play it.

- Take some time to study your game after a round. Where can you improve your game? Where did you use poor judgment in playing a shot? The number of putts you take for a round is an important part of your game. Record the putts for each hole by placing a small number in one corner of the square for the score for each hole.

- Prepare to play a good game of golf. Warm up by hitting some practice shots or by exercises and swinging the club. Try to develop some feeling of relaxation before you start your round. The greatest area of tension for anyone is through the neck and shoulders. Make some movements and stretches that will relax these areas. A good yawn is relaxing. As you play your round of golf, stay "easy" so you can use your muscles efficiently when you strike the ball.

Essential Knowledge 10

If you are a novice you cannot expect to hit the ball like the experienced player, but you can put yourself in his class in some respects. You can gain knowledge of the game and practice correct procedures of conduct. You can become "well-informed." Supplement the following information by studying the official rule book and other golf books, and by carefully observing experienced players on the course. Be willing and ready to learn, and you will be a welcome member of any golfing group.

Etiquette

The rules of etiquette are not strict formalities that complicate play. They simplify and enhance the game. Observance of these rules makes it possible to play better golf and enjoy the game more, to keep the course in good playing condition, and to allow more people to play golf by speeding up play.

Playing good golf requires concentration. Etiquette and good sportsmanship thus require that you respect and do not distract the player making a stroke. Always stand quietly and out of range of the player when he is addressing the ball or taking a stroke. Do not stand directly behind the ball or directly behind the hole.

Care of the Golf Course

1. Replace any divot and press it firmly in place. Avoid taking divots with practice swings.
2. Walk carefully on the putting green to avoid marring the surface. Do not step or stand at the edge of the hole (cup).
3. Do not drop or throw the flagstick on the green.
4. If you use a golf cart, keep it well away from the apron of the putting green.
5. If your ball makes a pit mark on the green, lift up the grass with a tee and press the grass back in place thus leaving a level surface.
6. When you lift your ball from the wrong putting green, drop it well off that green to avoid taking a chance of damaging the apron as you stroke the ball.
7. When leaving a bunker, smooth out the surface so that its condition is as good or better than when you entered it.

Playing Without Delay

1. When you pay your green fee, remember you are one of many paying for the privilege of playing on the course.
2. Be ready to play. Have a knowledge of safety, etiquette, and rules and possess basic skills in the strokes.
3. Any instruction on the course should be incidental. There should not be any delay because one person is attempting to teach another.
4. You will need your own set of clubs, golf bag, balls, and tees. Do not borrow clubs from another player. Carry your own golf bag. Do not be burdened with extra items such as purses and sweaters. Place them in the golf bag or check them at the pro shop.
5. Avoid delaying play by taking numerous practice swings.
6. Be ready to take your stroke when it is your turn. It is possible to plan ahead for some strokes. (See Chapter 7—Putting.)
7. Identify your ball before starting play. Check to see that you are not playing the same make and ball number as another player in your group. When your ball is in play, as on the fairway, do not pick up the ball for identification. Simply look around it and check the make and number. If it appears that a player in the distance is going to play your ball by mistake, call "fore" and wave to him.
8. When you hit a ball, spot its position carefully. Spot its position in relation to some stationary object so you can walk directly to it. Watch the stroke results of other players in your group so you can help in any search for a ball.
9. As a novice, if you find yourself in some difficult situation, e.g., unable to hit from a deep bunker after making several attempts, pick up the ball and drop it out of the bunker. Your scores for your early games of golf are not so important that they merit your delaying the play of others.
10. When your ball is on the wrong fairway, let players playing that hole have the right of way. Some courses have a local rule allowing you to lift the ball from the wrong fairway and drop it in the correct fairway. Safety and speeding up play make this an acceptable local rule.
11. If your group is delaying play by failing to keep its place, losing more than one clear hole on the players in front, invite the following group to pass. In turn, if you are extended this courtesy, express your appreciation.
12. When someone in your group is searching for his ball, help in the search. Invite following players to play through.

On the Putting Green

1. Place golf bag or cart well off and at the side of the green nearest the next tee.
2. Allow the player farthest from the hole to play first, whether he be on or off the putting surface.
3. Do not step or stand in any line of play. Do not allow your shadow to be cast in someone's line of play.

4. Mark and lift your ball when requested to do so. To mark your ball's position, place a small coin or marker behind the ball as you lift it. If your ball is in a direct line of play, measure the necessary lengths of the putter head to one side of the line and place the coin at this spot.
5. When holding the flagstick, stand to one side of the hole and hold both the stick and the pennant. The stick should be held in the hole until removal is necessary. After removal, lay the flagstick down out of play. When all players are on the putting green or close to it, the player whose ball is closest to the hole generally offers to attend the flagstick.
6. When all players have holed out, replace the flagstick, leave the green immediately, and proceed to the next tee. There are safety reasons for this admonition as well as other obvious reasons. Do not stand on the green after completion of play either to review play of the hole or to mark your scores on the score card.

In the Bunker (Sand Trap)

1. Leave the bag or cart well outside the edge of the bunker.
2. Enter the bunker at the lowest bank and take the shortest route to the ball.
3. Do not enter or stand in a bunker when another player is playing from it.
4. On leaving the bunker, smooth out all footprints and marks which you have made.

Rules*

This is a summary of certain rules. This knowledge together with the rules of etiquette will enable you to play golf properly, but it is no substitute for the official rules.

Types of Competition

Some rules differ for the two types of competition, *stroke play* and *match play*. Most golf played is stroke play. In this competition the winner is the person with the lowest score for the stipulated number of rounds, usually four rounds, a total of 72 holes. In case players are tied for the low score at the end of the tournament, the U.S.G.A. recommends that these players play another 18 hole round to determine the winner. The terms "competitor" and "fellow competitor" are used to describe the players in stroke play.

Match play competition is based on scores for each hole, not total score for a round. In a match a person competes against only one other player, his opponent. They play until one person is more holes ahead than there are holes remaining to be played in the match. If the match is tied at the end of a round, the players continue play until one player wins a hole. Match play is an elimination type tournament, so in the final round there are only two players remaining to compete for the championship.

*The official rules may be obtained from your local golf club or from the U.S.G.A., 40 East 38th St., New York, N.Y. 10016.

Match Play Score Card

Assume that at the end of nine holes Bill is 1 hole up on Joe. Hole #10 is tied or *halved*. Bill remains 1 up. Joe wins #11. The match is *all square*. Joe wins #12 and #13. Joe is 2 up. Hole #14 is halved. Joe wins #15. Joe is *dormie* 3. A player is dormie when he is the same number of holes up as there are holes remaining to be played. Hole #16 is halved. Joe wins the match, 3 holes up with 2 remaining, or simply 3 and 2, (3-2).

HOLE NO.	10	11	12	13	14	15	16	17	18
Bill (1 up)	5	5	4	7	4	4	4	⊥	
	o	—	—	—	o	—	o		
Joe (1 down)	5	3	3	5	4	3	4	⊥	
	o	+	+	+	o	+	o		

Figure 50—Match Play Card

Rules for Teeing Off

1. Play is started on each hole by teeing the ball within the limits of the teeing area. This area is bounded in front by two tee markers and extends two club lengths back of the markers.
2. If in addressing the ball you accidentally knock it off the tee, you may replace it without penalty.
3. Honor, the privilege of teeing first, is decided by lot on the first tee. After the first hole, the honor is decided by scores on the previous hole. The person with the lowest score plays first and the rest follow according to scores. If players have the same scores then the player who previously had the honor continues to tee ahead of other players.

General Rules

1. After teeing off you continue striking the ball until you hole out. The ball should be played as it lies and not be touched except to strike it, unless situations or rules require or allow you to do otherwise.
2. You play in turn so the ball farthest from the hole is played first.
3. Any attempt to hit the ball is counted as a stroke, whether or not the ball is struck.
4. If you accidentally move the ball in play or cause it to move, this counts as a stroke.
5. If such loose impediments as fallen leaves and pebbles interfere with your play of the ball, you may move them, but they may *not* be moved from a hazard.
6. When the ball is in play, you cannot press or stamp down the ground near the ball or break or bend anything growing.
7. If your ball lies within two club lengths of an immovable obstruction, such as a ball washer, bench, or protective screen, you may lift the ball and drop it with no penalty. (See #8 following)
8. To drop a ball, stand facing the hole and drop the ball back over your shoulder. The ball must not be dropped nearer the hole.
9. If your ball comes to rest on the wrong putting green, you *must* lift the ball and drop it off the green, without penality.
10. If your ball lies in casual water, ground under repair, or in a hole made by a burrowing animal, you may lift the ball and drop it with-

out penalty. If casual water interferes with your play on the putting green, after lifting the ball you *place* the ball free of the water rather than dropping it.

11. You may ask only your caddie, partner, or partner's caddie for advice regarding the playing of a stroke.
12. If another player's ball interferes with your play, you may request that he mark and lift the ball.
13. There is some difference in the penalties for the breach of a rule. (See the official rule book.) The general penalty for breaking a rule is two strokes in stroke play and loss of hole in match play. (See #5 and #6 above.) If you remove loose impediments from a hazard or stamp down the grass back of the ball in play, it will cost you two strokes in stroke play, and you will immediately lose the hole in match play.
14. The score card should be checked for local rules and interpretations which apply to the course being played.

Rules for the Putting Green

1. When playing your ball on the putting green, request that the flagstick be attended or removed from the hole. The penalty for your ball striking the flagstick is two strokes in stroke play and loss of hole in match play.
2. In stroke play, when you play your ball on the putting green and your ball strikes a fellow competitor's ball, also on the putting green, the penalty is two strokes. If this impact moves the fellow competitor's ball, he must replace it.
3. In match play, if your ball strikes your opponent's ball there is no penalty. Your opponent has the option of replacing his ball or leaving it where it comes to rest.

Rules for Hazards

1. By U.S.G.A. definition there are two types of hazards: bunkers and water hazards. A bunker usually is a depressed area of bare ground covered with sand, frequently called a sand trap. Grass covered area surrounding the bunker is not part of the hazard. The grass covered area or any dry ground surrounding a water hazard may be part of the hazard. Local rules will define the limits of water hazards.
2. Loose impediments may not be moved from a hazard.
3. Man-made objects, such as a rake, may be moved.
4. In addressing the ball in a hazard, you may *not* ground the club. You may *not* touch the surface of the hazard with the clubhead before taking your forward swing to strike the ball.
5. If you lose a ball in a water hazard or find it impossible to play, you may drop a ball any distance back of the hazard keeping the spot at which the ball last crossed the hazard between you and the hole, and add one penalty stroke. If the ball was hit from the tee into the hazard, you have the option of re-teeing a ball and adding one penalty stroke.

For a lateral water hazard there is an optional procedure. Under penalty of one stroke, you may drop a ball within 2 club lengths of either side of the hazard, opposite the point where the ball last crossed the hazard, but not nearer the hole.

Ball in Water Hazard

In situation A it is to your advantage to tee the ball again. In situation B, you would lose too much yardage if you played again from the tee. Thus, usually you would drop a ball any distance back of the hazard keeping the spot at which the ball last crossed the margin of the hazard between you and the hole. (Note Drop Area, Figure 51.) You may choose a nice grassy area upon which to drop the ball, providing all other provisions of the rule are followed.

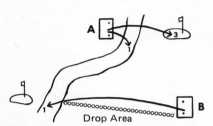

Figure 51—Ball In the Water Hazard

Ball Out of Bounds, Lost or Unplayable

1. A ball is out of bounds when it lies on ground on which play is prohibited. The area is usually marked by a fence or out of bounds stakes.
2. You are allowed five minutes to search for a ball. After that time the ball is deemed lost.
3. You are the sole judge as to when your ball is unplayable.
4. The penalty for out of bounds, lost ball, and unplayable ball is loss of distance and one stroke. The player must play his next stroke at the spot from which the original ball was played and add one penalty stroke. (See #5.)
5. If the ball is unplayable, there is an optional rule. Under a penalty of one stroke the ball may be dropped either within 2 club lengths of the unplayable position but not nearer the hole; or the ball may be dropped any distance behind the point where the ball lay, keeping that point between yourself and the hole.
6. When you hit a ball that you think might be out of bounds or lost, you may hit a provisional ball before you proceed toward the hole. If the original ball is playable, you play it and pick up the provisional ball. If the original ball is out of bounds or lost, then you continue play with the provisional ball.

Stroke and Distance Rule (See Figure 52)

A player drives out of bounds (1). He tees another ball, adds a penalty stroke and shoots 3 from the tee. From the fairway he shoots his fourth shot into the rough and loses the ball. He drops a ball at spot (X), adds a penalty stroke and shoots stroke 6.

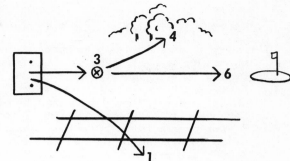

Figure 52—Stroke and
Distance Rule

Handicaps

A handicap is a number representing approximately the strokes a player shoots over par for a round. For instance, if a player has a handicap of 2, he is an excellent golfer; if he has a handicap of 25, he is a novice. A player who has a handicap of 0 averages near par and is called a scratch golfer.

To establish a handicap* a given number of rounds are played, usually 20. Score cards are turned in to the golf club or association and the handicap is figured from the 10 lowest scores of the 20.

Handicaps are used to equalize competitive play. In an 18 hole stroke play handicap event, a net score is computed for each player by subtracting his handicap from the actual (gross) score. The player with the low net score is the winner.

In match play the player with the higher handicap is allowed to subtract from his score on certain holes. For example, two opponents have handicaps of 7 and 4. The player with the 7 handicap subtracts one stroke from each of his scores on the three holes with a handicap rating of 1, 2, and 3. On the score card shown in the text, the three holes rated most difficult are #6, #14, and #9 for men, and #3, #17, and #5 for women. The player with the handicap of 4 spots the 7 handicapper one stroke on each of these holes, if the full handicap difference is allowed.

Honest and up-to-date handicaps make competition between players of unequal ability possible and enjoyable.

Selection of Equipment and Accessories

The amount of money you wish to invest in golf will determine your selection of equipment and accessories. Your initial investment can be a small one or a considerable one. Used sets of clubs and used golf balls are available, and minimum sets of new clubs and new balls are marketed at reasonable prices. A variety of new, high quality matched sets of clubs offer a wide selection to the person wishing to make a substantial investment in clubs. Generally the more expensive clubs will have more "feel." Higher quality material is used in their construction, and the time is taken to match the shafts and clubheads to insure better balance. Whether the

---

*For detailed information on handicapping and tournaments write the U.S.G.A. for *Golf Committee Manual and USGA Handicap System.*

STROKE PLAY AND MATCH PLAY—WHAT IS THE RULE?

1. Failing to play according to honor on the tee; playing out of turn on the fairway.
2. Driving from outside the limits of the teeing area.
3. Breaking off the limb of a tree which interferes with play.
4. Stamping down the turf back of a ball in play.
5. Removing fallen leaves from a sand trap.
6. A ball played from the putting green strikes the flagstick; strikes another ball on the putting green.
7. Playing a wrong ball from the rough; from the bunker.

clubs be moderately priced or expensive, it is important that the clubs fit you. If you buy clubs from a trained, experienced golf professional or salesperson, you can expect to be fitted with the correct clubs.

Because of the differences in height, strength, and hand size between men and women, men's clubs are longer, have stronger and stiffer shafts, have larger grips, and are heavier. The average golfer will find the medium shaft best suits his needs. The person with above average power and strength might find a shaft stiffer than medium better, while a person with average or less strength and power may be helped by a more flexible shaft. The weight of clubs can vary considerably. A recent concept in fitting clubs is to consider the swing weight of the clubs. Simply stated, swing weight is a measurement of the clubhead weight in proportion to the shaft and grip weight. This weight is given by letter and number. The swing weight of women's clubs ranges from C-0 to C-9. C-0 to C-2 is a light club, C-3 to C-6 is a medium club and C-7 to C-9 is a heavier club. Swing weights of D-0 to D-1 are light clubs for most men, D-2 and D-3 medium, and D-4 to D-6 heavy. A special scale is used to measure swing weight. There is nothing on the club to indicate the total weight or the swing weight of a club. A golf professional can check the over-all and swing weight of clubs for you.

The golf bag you select will probably depend on the number of clubs you will carry and whether you will carry your clubs and bag on your shoulder or pull them on a cart. Hand golf carts to carry equipment are popular accessory items. They are also available for rent at most courses. The electric carts have changed the game of golf considerably for some people, because walking need no longer be a prominent part of the game.

Wearing either a golf glove on the left hand or gloves on both hands will prevent blisters and callouses forming on the hands, and also may help in holding the club. You will need to wear comfortable, flat heeled oxfords that lace. Golf shoes with spikes are preferred for these will help you maintain balance in swinging and also will make walking on the course easier. Golf gloves and golf shoes are not absolutely necessary for your golf, but they are both recommended. Hats or visors for protection from the sun are also recommended.

Comfortable and appropriate sports clothes should be worn for golf. An attractive outfit for women is a straight line skirt and sports shirt or sweater, or a shirtwaist dress. For men, slacks and a sports shirt or sweater is the most popular dress. Bermuda length shorts worn with sports shirts or sweaters have become popular attire for both men and women.

You and the Game of Golf

Are You Ready to Attempt Play on the Course?

1. Have you developed some consistency in hitting the ball with the full swing? Do you know the distances you can get with the various clubs?
2. Have you practiced hitting different distances with the medium and short irons? Have you learned how much to "choke up" on the grip and how much swing to take for given distances?
3. Have you practiced putting so that in most longer putts of 25 feet or more you can hole out in 2 putts? Are you able to sink many putts of 1 to 2 feet in length?
4. Have you carefully studied and learned the safety precautions, etiquette, and the rules? Are you willing to watch the conduct of the experienced golfer and to learn from these observations?

Tips for Your Early Experience on the Course

1. If available, play a course consisting of short holes. If you play a full length course, plan to play less than 18 holes at a time when the course is not crowded.
2. If possible, have an experienced golfer guide you in correct conduct.
3. You will most likely take more strokes than the experienced golfer. Be willing to make up this time by walking rapidly between shots.
4. Don't be concerned with your scores. Become oriented to the course and follow correct procedure.
5. If you are in a difficult situation that may hold up play, consider possible solutions. For instance: finding it impossible to hit from deep rough—pick up your ball, toss it into the fairway and continue play; taking many putts on the green—pick up your ball and discontinue play of this hole.
6. Golf is a complicated game. Be patient. Consider other players. With experience, study, and practice you soon will be playing golf as it should be played.

Golf Conduct

The test of a player is: Does he really play golf? One might think this a ridiculous question. However, golfing authorities are becoming increasingly critical of and concerned with present playing practices. Some people play under the guise: "I play for the fun of it." They do not choose to meet the challenges of the game by playing according to the rules; they have little or no consideration either for their fellow players or the golf course. Although in the minority, their number is great enough to detract from the game and their actions deserve censure. It is hoped that you who have read this text will make some contribution to correcting these poor practices and to preserving the fine traditions of the game.

The Measure of a Golfer

- He meets the challenges of the game. He plays by the rules. The rules are self-enforced.
- He is aware of sharing the course with other players. He realizes the importance of keeping his place on the course so as not to hold up the play of golfers following.
- He follows practices that will help keep the course in the best possible condition.
- He observes the safety precautions and the etiquette to the finest degree, thereby making play most enjoyable for himself and for all players.

May your participation in this fine pastime be one of success and pleasure. May your participation and actions show your appreciation of the course and contribute to the recreation and pleasure of all golfers.

Glossary of Terms

Addressing the ball: Taking the grip and stance in preparation to making a stroke.

All square: A term used in match play to indicate the match is tied.

Approach shot: A stroke played to the putting green.

Apron: The area surrounding the putting green.

Away: The ball lying farthest from the hole.

Backspin: A reverse spin of the ball in the vertical plane.

Barranca: A deep ravine. (Spanish)

Bite: The backspin on the ball causing it to stop upon landing on the ground.

Birdie: A score of one under par for a hole.

Bogey: Commonly used to describe a score of one over par for a hole.

Brassie: The #2 wood.

Break of green: The slant or slope of the putting green.

Bunker: Usually a depressed area covered with sand, commonly called a sand trap.

Caddie: A person who carries the clubs and otherwise assists a player as the rules provide.

Casual water: A temporary accumulation of water not recognized as a hazard.

Chip shot: A short, low shot played to the putting green. Also run-up shot.

Cup: The hole on the putting green, 4 1/4 inches in diameter and at least 4 inches deep.

Curtis Cup Matches: International team matches between women amateurs of Great Britain and the United States.

Divot: A piece of turf cut or displaced in making a stroke. Should be replaced and pressed down.

Dog leg: A hole in which the fairway curves to the right or left.

Dormie: A term used in match play. A player is dormie when he is as many holes up as there are holes remaining to be played.

Double bogey: A term in common use to describe a score of two over par for a hole.

Double eagle: A score of three under par for a hole.

Driver: The #1 wood.

Dub: An unskilled golfer, or to hit a poor shot.

Duffer: A player with poor skill.

x *Eagle:* A score of two under par for a hole.

Explosion shot: A shot played from a sand trap. An attempt is made to swing the club through the sand well back of the ball.

Fade: A shot that curves to the right in flight.

x *Fairway:* The mowed grassy area between the tee and putting green.

Fat shot: A shot in which the ground is struck before contacting the ball, usually resulting in a poor shot.

Fellow competitor: The person with whom you play in stroke play.

x*Flagstick:* The marker which indicates location of the hole.

Flat swing: A swing in which the club is swung in a low arc. At the top of the backswing the club shaft is lower than the usual orthodox swing.

Flub: A poorly hit shot, or to hit a poor shot.

\ *Fore!:* A warning cry to anyone who might be endangered by a golf shot.

- *Foursome:* Four players playing together who may or may not be engaged in a match.

Frog hair: The grass surrounding the putting green.

Gross score: The actual total score for a round.

- *Grounding the club:* Placing the sole of the club on the ground in preparation for making the stroke.

Halved or halving a hole: In match play, to tie a hole.

_ *Handicap:* The approximate number of strokes one shoots over par, or the allowance of strokes to equalize players of different ability.

x*Hazard:* By U.S.G.A. definition, bunkers and water hazards.

High handicapper: A player who shoots many strokes over par, an unskilled player.

Hole high: The ball is in a position as far as the hole but off to either side of it.

Hole out: To complete the play of a hole.

x *Hook:* A ball that curves in flight to the left due to a horizontal, counterclockwise spin on the ball.

x *Honor:* The privilege of hitting first from the tee.

In 9: The second 9 holes of an 18 hole course.

L.P.G.A.: Ladies Professional Golf Association of America.

Lateral Water Hazard: A water hazard running approximately parallel to the line of play.

x *Lie:* The position of the ball on the ground.

x *Loft of club:* The angle of pitch of the club face.

Loose impediments: Objects such as dead grass and fallen leaves, pebbles, worms, fallen twigs, etc.

Low handicapper: A skilled golfer who shoots near par.

Mashie: The #5 iron.

x*Match play:* Competition based on scores for each hole rather than total score.

Medal play: More commonly called stroke play. Competition by total score.

Medalist: The player with the lowest score for a qualifying round of a match play tournament.

Mid-iron: The #2 iron.

Mixed foursome: A group of four players made up of two women and two men.

- *Mulligan:* An illegal practice of taking a second drive from the first tee if the first shot is a poor one.

Nassau scoring system: A system of scoring allowing one point to the winner of each 9 holes and one point for the match.

Net score: A score resulting from subtracting the handicap from the gross score.

Niblick: The #9 iron.

Obstruction: An artificial object on the course which may be movable or fixed.

Open tournament: A competitive event in which both amateurs and professionals play, such as the United States National Open and the British Open.

Opponent: The player opposing you in a match.

Out 9: The first 9 holes of an 18 hole course.

Out of Bounds: Ground on which play is prohibited, usually marked by out of bounds stakes or fences.

P.G.A.: Men's Professional Golf Association.

Par: An arbitrary standard of scoring excellence based on the length of a hole and allowing two putts on the putting green.

Pin high: Same as hole high.

Pitch shot: A shot played to the putting green that travels in a high trajectory.

Press: Attempting to hit the ball beyond one's normal power.

Pronation: An anatomical term to describe the turning of the hand and forearm inward. Supination is the opposite action in which the hand and forearm are turned out so the palm is facing up.

Provisional ball: A second ball played in case the first ball is or is thought to be lost or out of bounds.

Pull: A shot that travels to the left of the intended line.

Push: A shot that travels in a straight line, but to the right of the intended target.

Rough: The areas bordering the fairway in which the grass and weeds are allowed to grow.

Royal and Ancient Golf Club of St. Andrews, Scotland: The governing body for mens' golf in Great Britain.

Rub of green: An unpredictable happening to the ball when the ball in motion or at rest is stopped or deflected by an outside agency.

Ryder Cup Matches: Mens' professional team matches between Great Britain and the United States.

Sand trap: A term commonly used for a bunker.

Scotch foursome: A foursome of players in which two teams compete. Each team uses only one ball and the players alternate striking the ball.

Scratch player: A player who has a handicap of 0, shooting consistently near par.

Slice: A shot that curves in flight to the right, caused by the ball spinning in a horizontal, clockwise manner.

Spoon: The #3 wood.

Stance: The position of the feet in addressing the ball.

Stroke play: Competition by total strokes.

Stymie: To have another player's golf ball or some object blocking one's line of play—to be stymied. Also an obsolete rule of golf.

Summer golf: The official rules of golf which require the ball to be played from where it comes to rest on the fairway.

Tee: The starting place for a hole or the peg on which the ball is placed for driving.

Tee markers: The markers placed on the tee to indicate the forward limits of the teeing area.

Through the green: This is the whole of the course, except the teeing ground and putting green of the hole being played and all hazards.

Upright swing: A swing in which the club is swung high into the air on the backswing and follow-through. The opposite of flat swing.

U.S.G.A.: The United States Golf Association—the governing body of golf in the U.S.A.

Walker Cup Matches: Matches between men amateurs of Great Britain and the United States.

Winter rules: Special local rules which allow the ball to be moved to a better lie on the fairway; also called "preferred lies."

Index